*The American
Immigration Collection*

The
Legislative History
of Naturalization
in the United States

FRANK GEORGE FRANKLIN

Arno Press and The New York Times

NEW YORK 1969

The Legislative History of Naturalization
in the United States

The Legislative History *of* Naturalization *in the* United States

From the Revolutionary War to 1861

By

FRANK GEORGE FRANKLIN, Ph.D.

Professor of History and Political Science in the
University of the Pacific

Chicago
THE UNIVERSITY OF CHICAGO PRESS
1906

Composed and Printed By
The University of Chicago Press
Chicago, Illinois, U. S. A.

PREFACE

The subject of naturalization has assumed a larger importance in the history of the United States than in that of any other nation. In this study I have sought to exhibit the course of opinion thereon chiefly as it manifested itself in discussion, reports, and legislation at the central forum of American political life.

The sources of information are sufficiently indicated. In large measure I have let men speak for themselves. Some latitude of expression has been allowed in indirect quotation, in the effort to preserve the flavor of the original utterance.

I am indebted to Professor Frederick J. Turner, of the University of Wisconsin, for much helpful suggestion and criticism upon the earlier part of the work. I desire to mention Professors Hermann Edouard von Holst and Benjamin S. Terry, of the University of Chicago, because of inspiration that came from them. The work was begun with the encouraging approval of Dr. von Holst, and in anticipation of his invaluable criticism of which his sickness and death deprived me. The exceptional facilities of the library of the Wisconsin State Historical Society have lightened my task. The abundant courtesy of its officials calls for appreciative acknowledgment.

F. G. F.

TO VIOLA PRICE FRANKLIN

IN APPRECIATION OF HER HELP AND INSPIRATION

TABLE OF CONTENTS

CHAPTER   PAGE

I. THE REVOLUTIONARY PERIOD 1

II. THE CONVENTION OF 1787 19

III. THE ACT OF 1790 33

IV. THE ACT OF 1795 49

V. THE ACT OF 1798 72

VI. THE ACT OF 1802 97

VII. THE ACT OF 1813 117

VIII. AN ACT CONCERNING EVIDENCE 129

IX. EXPATRIATION 134

X. THE ACT OF 1824 167

XI. THE BEGINNINGS OF NATIVE AMERICANISM . 184

XII. THE PERIOD OF AGGRESSIVE NATIVE
AMERICANISM 215

XIII. THE PERIOD OF AGGRESSIVE NATIVE
AMERICANISM (*continued*) 247

XIV. THE KNOW-NOTHING PERIOD 278

BIBLIOGRAPHY 301

INDEX 307

CHAPTER I

THE REVOLUTIONARY PERIOD

The Declaration of Independence declared the right of the people to establish a new government. Yet earlier the Continental Congress had exercised authority to declare certain Tories to be out of the protection of the United States, and had ordered that any person refusing its bills should be deemed an enemy of his country and be refused all intercourse with the inhabitants of the colonies.[1]

The early continental congresses required no oath from even their members. Soldiers at enlistment merely declared that they had voluntarily enlisted and did bind themselves to conform to the rules for the government of the army. Late in 1776 they were sworn "to be true to the United States of America and to serve them honestly and faithfully."[2] Congress early resolved "that no oath by way of test be . . . . required of any of the inhabitants of these colonies, by any military officers."[3] A law of January 3, 1776, required certain officers of the government, chiefly

[1] *Journals of Congress,* II, 8, 21; January 11, 1776.
[2] *Ibid.,* I, 118; II, 367.
[3] *Ibid.,* II, 88.

I

those in charge of funds and supplies, to take an oath truly and faithfully to discharge their duties.[4]   Congress later [5] established an oath for all officers in the continental service and for all holding civil office from Congress, as follows:

I ——— do acknowledge the Thirteen United States of America, namely, ... , to be free, independent and sovereign states, and declare that the people thereof owe no allegiance or obedience to George the Third, King of Great Britain; and I renounce, refuse, and abjure any allegiance or obedience to him: and I do swear that I will to the utmost of my power support, maintain and defend the said United States against the said King George, etc.[6]

Even before the adoption of the Declaration of Independence the Continental Congress defined the citizenship of the colonies. It resolved, June 6, 1776, while considering a report of its Committee on Spies, "that all persons abiding within any of the United Colonies and deriving protection from the laws of the same owe allegiance to the said laws, and are members of such colony." Persons only temporarily in a colony were declared to owe allegiance to it during their temporary stay, and it was made treason for such to levy war.[7]

[4] *Op. cit.*, I, 187.

[5] October 21, 1776; February 3, 1778.

[6] *Journals of Congress*, II, 426. January 16, 1777, Congress ordered that the oath of fidelity be published (*ibid.*, III, 20).

[7] *Ibid.*, II, 229.

Hamilton accepted this position, and developed its application to those who had been within the British lines during the war, and to Tories generally, in his *Letters from Phocion,* written in 1784. In opposition to proposed New York legislation hostile to Tories, he pleaded both their legal status and their treaty rights. The treaty, he held, forbade attainting individuals for war crimes, and for the state to disfranchise or punish whole classes of its citizens by general descriptions and without a trial was tyranny. To say, on the other hand, that by espousing the cause of Great Britain the Tories became aliens, and that it would satisfy the treaty to confine them to the privileges of aliens, was to admit that subjects might at pleasure renounce their allegiance to the state of which they were members and devote themselves to a foreign jurisdiction. That was a principle contrary to law, and subversive of government; also it would lead to forfeiture of property by a fraudulent subterfuge that was more odious than an open violation of the treaty. The state could not deprive a citizen of his right without an offense ascertained by a trial, and the treaty forbade prosecution and trial.

The idea of suffering the Tories to live among us under disqualifications is equally mischievous and absurd. It is necessitating a large body of citizens in the State to continue enemies to the government.

By the Declaration of Independence, acceded to by the New York convention, July 9, 1776, the late colony of New York became an independent state. All the inhabitants who were subjects under the former government, and who did not withdraw themselves upon the change which took place, were to be considered as citizens owing allegiance to the new government. This, at least, is the legal presumption; and this was the principle in fact, upon which all the measures of our public councils have been grounded.[8]

Thus, according to Hamilton, residents of New York, formerly British citizens, had the opportunity of making choice of American or British citizenship immediately after July 9, 1776. By choosing the latter they chose to become alien enemies in the place of their residence, and were under the necessity of withdrawing from the state. Persons who remained were, and continued to be, American citizens, although the fortunes of war later left them within the enemy's lines, where they owed a temporary and qualified obedience, and although they took voluntary part with the enemy and became traitors thereby. He held that the idea of citizens transforming themselves into aliens by taking part against their state was altogether unknown and inadmissible.

[8] Lodge, *Works of Alexander Hamilton,* III, 449-70.

Bancroft states the theory of citizenship resulting from the Declaration of Independence thus: He that had owed primary allegiance to Great Britain now owed primary allegiance to the United States, but it was no treason to adhere to the king's government. Yet those who chose to remain on the soil, by residence accepted the protection of the new government, and have owed it allegiance. He adds that this was why for twelve years in American state papers "free inhabitants" and "citizens" were convertible terms, either or both being used.[9]

During the Revolutionary War repeated efforts were made to detach the foreign element from the British army by offers of land and citizenship. First, in August, 1776, Congress adopted the report of a committee to devise plans for encouraging the Hessians and other foreigners to quit the British service. They declared it to have been

the wise policy of these states to extend the protection of their laws to all those who should settle among them of whatever nation or religion they might be and to admit them to a participation of the benefits of civil and religious freedom.

They asserted that the "benevolence" and "salutary effects" of this practice advocated its continuance. They resolved that

[9] Bancroft, *History of the United States*, V, 200.

these states will receive all such foreigners who shall leave the armies [of England] . . . . and shall chuse to become members of any of these states; and they shall be . . . . invested with the rights, privileges and immunities of natives as established by the laws of these states.

Each of them should be given fifty acres of land. A little later (August 27, 1776) they resolved to give lands, proportioned in amount to their rank, to foreign officers that should leave the British army "and chuse to become citizens of these states." Again, two years later (April 15, 1778), they said to such foreign officers and soldiers: "We are willing to receive you with open arms into the bosom of our country." [10]

Jefferson, as governor of Virginia, issued a proclamation, February 2, 1781, in which he recited the offer of Congress of fifty acres of land to foreigners who should leave the British army "and should chuse to become members of any of these states." He had thought fit, by and with the advice of his council, to make more generally known that engagement of Congress, and to promise further "to all such Foreigners who shall leave the armies of his Britannic Majesty while in this state, and repair forthwith to me at this place," that he should recommend the further

[10] *Journals of Congress*, II, 310, 330; *Secret Journals of Congress*, I, 70.

donation to each of two cows, and their exemption, during the existing war and their continuance in the state, from all taxes for the support of the war, and from military service.[11]

Opinions vary as to the result of these overtures. Of 29,867 Germans sent to America, 12,554 were not returned at the end of the war. It is estimated that five thousand of these had deserted, largely while prisoners of war. Some of them were enlisted in the American army against the wishes of Washington. German writers claim that the Germans deserted less freely than did the English soldiers.[12] The Gloucester (Eng.) *Journal* of November 10, 1783, in a dispatch of September 10, from Kingston, Jamaica, relates that four thousand British prisoners of war were received in New York from Philadelphia, among whom were about seven hundred Germans, all that could be found out of nine thousand of those people, who have been made prisoners by the Americans in the course of the war; the remainder have dispersed themselves in the different provinces, and have been naturalized by Congress,[13] in order to forward the manufactures, agriculture, and population of their extensive territories.

After making allowance for escaping prisoners, and for deaths from wounds and disease, per-

[11] Ford, *Writings of Jefferson,* II, 445.
[12] Lowell, *The Hessians in the Revolution,* 285, 290, 291, 300.
[13] This, of course, is a mistake.

haps this estimate of the number of deserters does not vary greatly from the former one.

Other acts of Congress include a provision for passports to certain inhabitants of New Providence certifying their fidelity "and design to remove . . . . to . . . . states . . . . with intent to become subject to the same;" [14] a recommendation to Maryland to assemble the inhabitants in certain counties on an appointed day and take the oath of allegiance required by the state, disarming all that refused it;[15] a recommendation to New York to receive as citizens certain Canadian and other refugees (eighty men and women besides children) who had petitioned Congress from Fishkill, N. Y.;[16] a resolution to confirm their possessions to French settlers at Post St. Vincents (Vincennes, Ind.) who before 1783 "had professed themselves citizens of the United States or any of them." [17]

A remarkable proposition is contained in a letter from John Adams at Paris to the president of Congress, as follows:

There is another point of very great importance, which I am persuaded will be aimed at by the English ministers; I am sure it will be by the people of England, whenever

[14] *Secret Journals of Congress,* I, 87; August 17, 1778.
[15] *Journals of Congress,* III, 36; February 1, 1777.
[16] *Ibid.,* VIII, 236; August 9, 1783.
[17] *Ibid.,* XIII, 91.

terms of peace shall be talked. For facilitating the return
of commerce they will wish to have it stipulated by the
treaty, that the subjects of Great Britain shall have the
rights of citizens in America, and the citizens of the United
States the rights of subjects in the British dominions.
Some of the consequences of such an agreement to them
and to us are obvious and very important; but they are so
numerous, and it is so difficult to determine whether the
benefits or inconveniences prevail, that I should be sorry to
have so great a question left to my determination.[18]

The same result was sought in 1794 by
Lord Loughborough (the former Wedder-
burn, now lord chancellor) in a proposal "that
in either country, the subjects or citizens of
the other shall be exempted from all the disabili-
ties of alienage." John Quincy Adams wrote
of this in his diary:

The article proposed by Lord Loughborough, the chancellor, is certainly extremely liberal; although Mr. Jay
thinks it best to leave it as a subject for future consideration. . . . . Such an Article would certainly tend to pro-
mote the friendly intercourse between the Nations; and I
do not know that it could produce any material incon-
venience to either. But it would be necessary to have an
Act of Parliament to confirm the stipulation here, which,
his Lordship says, may be obtained without difficulty. A
more material obstacle arises from the constitution of the
United States, with one clause of which such an article
would certainly militate.

The provision referred to is doubtless that
giving to Congress the power of establishing

[18] John Adams, *Works*, VII, 136; March 24, 1780.

a uniform rule of naturalization. That this
is the case is shown by the comment of Adams
upon the Louisiana Purchase. He regarded
it as abolishing the Constitution by treaty,
and one of his counts against it was: "It nat-
uralizes foreign nations in a mass."[19] Adams
saw in this proposition support for Loughborough's professions of very friendly disposition toward the United States, although he
had been known as a conspicuous opponent
of America during the Revolution.[20]

There is a reference to a part of the same
question in an interview in 1817 between
Adams as minister to England and Hamilton,
a British under-secretary of state, in regard
to a claim for inheritance of land. Hamilton
had said that he found great difficulty in admitting a whole nation, eight millions of foreigners, to all the privileges of British subjects without having any claim upon their
allegiance. Adams replied that the

mere privilege of holding lands would never, in the present
condition of the world, have consequences important to
either government, and there was something very harsh in
stripping individuals of their estates on the mere ground of
alienage.[21]

This remarkable proposal has been revived
in England in recent years. Professor Dicey,

[19] J. Q. Adams, *Memoirs*, V, 400.

[20] *Ibid.*, I, 49; October 22, 1794.   [21] *Ibid.*, iii, 513.

of the chair of English law at Oxford University, in a notable lecture at All Souls College, while the arbitration treaty between the United States and England was before the United States Senate, earnestly advocated a common citizenship for British and Americans. He designed nothing in the least resembling political unity; but would merely have every American citizen, on landing at Liverpool, occupy the same position as to civil and political rights as the inhabitant of Victoria who might land from the same boat; and an Englishman, on landing in America, should enjoy the same civil and political rights as an American born and reared abroad who might first land there at the same time. The plan was wholly feasible. The practical effects would be comparatively small, but wholly good. The indirect and moral effects would be greatly beneficial. The alien already possessed in both countries nearly all the civil rights of citizens. The political status of the American when in England would become precisely that of his grandfather, who was a citizen of New York, or Massachusetts, and a subject of the crown. He might vote, sit in Parliament or in the cabinet, and even aspire to the House of Lords. The dubious advantages of American restrictions on naturalization were not worth weighing against the serious advantages of a common citizenship.[22]

Franklin's sketch of Articles of Confederation of May 10, 1775, contains no reference to citizenship.[23] This is because independence was not yet planned for. The draft of August 12, 1776, shortly after the declaration, is in Dickinson's handwriting. Arts. VI and VII provide that the inhabitants of each colony shall always enjoy the same rights, liberties, privileges, immunities, and advantages in the other colonies *that they now have,* except as those rights are [may be] limited by the further provision that the inhabitants of each colony shall enjoy [only] all rights of local and foreign trade in any other colony that the natives of such other colony enjoy. This reserved to each colony the privilege of enforcing upon the inhabitants of the other colonies such restrictions upon trade rights as it might propose for its own members.[24] With the matter thus before them, it is strange that the draft of the committee of the whole (August 20, 1776) contains no reference to the subject.[25] Ten weeks later Congress added the provision that

[22] New York *Nation,* LXIV, 198, Correspondence from Oxford.
[23] *Secret Journals of Congress,* I, 283.
[24] *Ibid.,* I, 292.   [25] *Ibid.,* I, 304.

the free inhabitants of each of these states, paupers, vagabonds, and fugitives from justice excepted, shall be entitled
to all privileges and immunities of free citizens in the
respective states; and the people of each state shall have
free ingress and regress to and from any other state;
and enjoy the same trade privileges as the inhabitants. The final text contained this
amendment with the word "respective"
changed to "several;" and reads as follows:

Art. IV. The better to secure and perpetuate mutual
friendship and intercourse among the people of the United
States in this Union, the free inhabitants of each of these
States, paupers, vagabonds, and fugitives from justice
excepted, shall be entitled to all privileges and immunities
of free citizens in the several States, and the people of each
State shall have free ingress and regress to and from any
other State, and shall enjoy therein all the privileges of
trade and commerce, subject to the same duties, impositions
and restrictions as the inhabitants thereof respectively,
provided that such restrictions shall not extend so far as
to prevent the removal of property imported into any State,
to any other State of which the owner is an inhabitant;
provided also, that no imposition, duties, or restriction
shall be laid by any State, on the property of the United
States, or either of them.

Among a number of points in a representation of the Legislature of New Jersey to Congress on the Articles of Confederation is the
objection that there is no oath or test to the
general government required of the members
of the Congress. Such an oath they thought
to be necessary. The Confederation Congress,

however, defeated a motion to amend the articles in accordance with this representation. Only three states were for it, six were against it, and one was divided.[26]

Madison said in *The Federalist:*

The dissimilarity in the rules of naturalization has long been remarked as a fault in our system, and as laying a foundation for intricate and delicate questions.

After quoting from the fourth article of the Confederation, he continues:

There is a confusion of language here, which is remarkable. Why the terms *free inhabitants* are used in one part of the article, *free citizen* in another, and *people* in another; or what was meant by superadding to "all privileges and immunities of free citizens," "all the privileges of trade and commerce," cannot easily be determined. It seems to be a construction scarcely avoidable, however, that those who come under the denomination of *free inhabitants* of a state, although not citizens of such a state, are entitled, in every other state, to all the privileges of *free citizens* of the latter; that is, to greater privileges than they may be entitled to in their own state: so that it may be in the power of a particular State, or rather every state is laid under a necessity, not only to confer the rights of citizenship in other States upon any whom it may admit to such rights within itself, but upon any whom it may allow to become inhabitants within its jurisdiction. But were an exposition of the term "inhabitants" to be admitted which would confine the stipulated privileges to citizens alone, the difficulty is diminished only, not removed. The very improper power would still be retained by each State, of

[26] *Elliott's Debates,* I, 87.

naturalizing aliens in every other State. In one State, residence for a short term confirms all the rights of citizenship; in another, qualifications of greater importance are required. An alien, therefore, legally incapacitated for certain rights in the latter, may, by previous residence only in the former, elude his incapacity; and thus the law of one State be preposterously rendered paramount to the law of another, within the jurisdiction of the other. We owe it to mere casualty, that very serious embarrassments on this subject have been hitherto escaped. By the laws of several States, certain descriptions of aliens, who had rendered themselves obnoxious, were laid under interdicts inconsistent not only with the rights of citizenship but with the privilege of residence. What would have been the consequence, if such persons, by residence or otherwise, had acquired the character of citizens under the laws of another State, and then asserted their rights as such, both to residence and citizenship, within the State proscribing them? Whatever the legal consequences might have been, other consequences would probably have resulted, of too serious a nature not to be provided against. The new Constitution has accordingly, with great propriety, made provision against them, and all others proceeding from the defect of the Confederation on this head, by authorizing the general government to establish a uniform rule of naturalization throughout the United States.[27]

Bancroft found in "intercitizenship and mutual equality of rights" of all members in the Confederation "a new character and an enduring unity," not found before in federations. Congress had at first defined only the membership of each colony. The Articles of

[27] *The Federalist*, No. XLII. Compare with the view of Bancroft, p. 5.

Confederation brought in the rule that membership might be transferred from one state to another.[28]   While there is here doubtless the original expression of this character by the lawmaking body common to the new union, and is perhaps a new quality in federations, yet there must be taken into account the earlier common English citizenship of the great majority of the members of the Confederation, and the common rights that it involved.   Those, whether continued or not throughout the preliminary states of their combination, must have done much to render intercitizenship in the federation inevitable. In other words, if here is a new character in federations, it is because this is a federation born out of conditions to which the new character was fundamental.   The intercitizenship of naturalized citizens was, on the other hand, not a matter of course.   There is little to show that their status in this respect had been worked out generally in either the colonial or the revolutionary period.   Colonial naturalization was usually limited in its benefits, by explicit provision, to the colony naturalizing.   This restriction was not made with reference to rights in other colonies.   It merely marked the limit of power under the

<hr />

[28] Bancroft, *History of the Constitution of the United States,* I, 118.

colony's charter, the act of 13 Geo. 2, or the veto power of governor and crown. England did not permit colonies to create English citizens, and often restrained them in the making of colonial citizens. A Virginian who was an Englishman, upon settling in Maryland, became a Marylander. There was no necessity for this result if he was a foreigner.

There is a case of naturalization, in the colonial period, first by Virginia and later by Maryland; and it seems probable from the record that the results of the Virginia naturalization were lost by the subsequent proceedings in Maryland. At any rate, the Virginia lands of one Dr. George Hacke, who was naturalized in Virginia in 1653, and again in Maryland in 1663, are said to have escheated at his death, and were regranted to his heirs, because he was a foreigner.[29] But, with the common tie one of their own formation, the rather anomalous condition that some of the citizens of one state should, and others should not, require naturalization upon removing to another state would naturally be done away with.

The transfer of citizenship from state to state provided for by the Articles of Confederation very soon led to complaints due to the

[29] *Virginia Historical Magazine*, V, 256.

easy naturalization laws of some of the states.
Edmund Randolph, writing to Madison, made
suggestions with reference to the intrusion
of obnoxious aliens through other states.
Madison replied (August 27, 1782) that his
hints merited attention, and that the subject
had been several times mentioned in Congress. He believed that no committee had
ever reported a remedy for the abuse, but
thought that a uniform rule of naturalization
ought certainly to be recommended to the
states. Their individual authority seemed, if
properly executed, to be competent to the
case of their own citizens.[30]   Many years
later in his introduction to the debates in the
convention, he wrote:

> Among the defects which had been severely felt was
> want of an uniformity in cases requiring it, as laws of
> naturalization and bankruptcy.[31]

[30] *Madison Papers*, I, 161. This seems to mean that states
may be left to control *state*, as distinguished from *federal*, citizenship.

[31] *Ibid.*, II, 712.

CHAPTER II

In the proceedings of the Constitutional Convention of 1787 we look for any traces of a new citizenship. The first of these is in the resolutions offered by Randolph on May 29. His sixth resolution,

that the national legislature ought to be empowered . . . . to legislate in all cases to which the separate states are incompetent, or in which the harmony of the United States may be interrupted by the exercise of individual legislation,

read in the light of the foregoing correspondence between Madison and Randolph, and the later proceedings of the convention, must be thought to comprehend consciously the subject in hand. His fourteenth resolution,

that the legislative, executive and judiciary powers, within the several states, ought to be bound, by oath, to support the articles of union,

is a step toward recognition of a new citizenship that met with considerable opposition.[1] That they contain nothing more strengthens the probability that resolution 6 was seen to be sufficiently inclusive to provide for federal naturalization.[2] These provisions were un-

[1] *Elliott's Debates*, I, 408; *Madison Papers*, V, 182f.
[2] *Elliott's Debates*, I, 143.

changed in the resolutions as amended and
agreed to in committee of the whole house
on June 19.

Meanwhile (June 15) Patterson's propositions were introduced and referred to a committee of the whole house, and they were debated the following day. The sixth of these
was identical with Randolph's fourteenth resolution. The tenth was:

Resolved, That the rule for naturalization ought to be
the same in every state.[3]

Pinckney's plan, long discredited, but recently in large measure rehabilitated, contains
nearly everything bearing on citizenship and
naturalization that found place in the final draft.
A later compromise plan communicated by Randolph to Madison July 10, but not introduced because the smaller states had succeeded in getting
an equal vote in all cases in the Senate, proposed
that each state should have one vote in that
branch in thirteen specified cases, one of which
was:

In regulating the rights to be enjoyed by citizens of
one state in the other states.[4]

Randolph's sixth and fourteenth resolutions were respectively the sixth and the
twentieth of the twenty-three resolutions ap-

---

[3] *Op. cit.*, I, 177.
[4] *Madison Papers*, II, 1110; III, Appendix, p. vii.

proved by the convention and referred to the Committee of Detail. Patterson's and Pinckney's resolutions were also laid before this committee.

The growth of the ideas that were embodied in the Constitution is to be studied further in the draft reported by this committee, in the revised draft made by the convention, in the final form as reported by the Committee on Style, and in the available reports of the proceedings and debates of the convention. I shall trace to its outcome each provision of the committee's draft that seems to require notice. The first of these leaves the qualifications for the federal suffrage to be determined by the several states, requiring only that they be the same as shall be established for electors to the lower branch of each state legislature. An effort to strike out the phrase by which "electors" was limited received the vote of Delaware only, probably because the change would tend to restrict a state to only one class of electors. The section passed unanimously as reported, and was not changed later.

Art. IV, sec. 2, read:

Every member of the House of Representatives . . . . shall have been a citizen in the United States for at least three years before his election.

"Citizen in" was changed to "citizen of." Various motions were made as to the number of years of citizenship to be required to qualify a representative. "Seven years" was inserted in place of "three years," with only Connecticut opposing. "Three years" was lost by a vote of 2 to 9. A motion for one year was lost, and the clause passed unanimously.[5] Some days later (August 13), extended discussion upon the term of citizenship to be required for senator having intervened, reconsideration was had. Wilson and Randolph moved to strike out "seven years" and insert "four years" as the requisite term of citizenship to qualify for the House of Representatives. Wilson thought it very proper for the electors to require seven years, but unnecessary and improper that the Constitution should chain them down to it. Gerry wished that in future eligibility might be confined to natives. Foreign powers would intermeddle and spend vast sums in secret service and in influencing the government. Williamson moved to require nine years of citizenship.

Hamilton was in general against embarrassing the government by minute restrictions. He proposed an amendment requiring

*Elliott's Debates, I, 224, 232.

only citizenship and inhabitancy. This would leave discretion to Congress, and answer every purpose. Madison, seconding the amendment, said that he wished to maintain a professed character of liberality, and to invite foreigners of merit and republican principles. America was indebted to immigration, and had advanced most rapidly where it was most encouraged. There was a possible danger in office, but it was by no means probable in any dangerous degree. The people would prefer natives. Wilson cited the rapid growth of Pennsylvania to a place among the foremost in population and prosperity as proof of the advantage of encouraging immigration. Almost all of her general officers in the Revolution were foreigners, and no complaint arose. Three of her deputies in this convention were not natives. He had no objection to Hamilton's motion, and withdrew his own. Butler was strenuous against foreigners in our councils. The vote on Hamilton's amendment was: ayes, 4 (Conn., Penn., Md., Va.); noes, 7 (N. H., Mass., N. J., Del., N. C., S. C., Ga.). On nine years the vote stood: ayes, 3 (N. H., S. C., Ga.), and noes, 8. Wilson renewed his motion for four years. It secured the votes of Conn., Md., and Va.

An amendment by Gouverneur Morris

opened up a new field for debate. He proposed the following:

Provided always, that the above limitation of seven years shall not be construed to affect the rights of those who are now citizens of the United States.

Mercer, in seconding this, said that it was necessary to prevent putting any who had become citizens below the level of natives. Rutledge thought that it might as well be said that all qualifications are disfranchisements, including the age qualification of twenty-five years. The policy of the precaution was as great for those now citizens as for those to become so.

Sherman held that the United States had not pledged equal privileges by invitations. Only individual states had done this. The United States were free to discriminate as they should judge it to be requisite. Gorham doubted the propriety of a retrospective restriction. When foreigners were naturalized, it would seem as if they stood on an equal footing with natives.

Madison found in the peculiar doctrine of Sherman a subtlety by which every national engagement might be evaded. Who but the states were to form the new Constitution? If it violated pledged faith, the states would be violators. Every state would be exposed to reproach, and reduced to the dilemma of rejecting the Constitution, or of violating the faith pledged to a part of its citizens. Gouverneur Morris denied that any pledge had been made to persons under twenty-five years, but faith had been pledged that foreigners should enjoy the privileges of citizens. Pinckney asserted that the laws of the states varied much as to naturalization, and that the United States could not be bound to respect them on such an occasion as this, when there was a sort of recurrence to first principles. Mason, too, was struck by the propriety, not the peculiarity, of Sherman's doctrine. There was need of greater caution at the beginning of the government, or there might be pernicious consequences in the commercial regulations. Wilson found in the provision of the Pennsylvania constitution, giving "all the rights whatsoever of citizens" to foreigners after two years' residence, together with the provision of the Articles of Confederation that citizens of one state should be citizens of all, an obligation resting upon Pennsylvania to maintain the faith thus pledged to her foreign-born citizens, and held that her failure would authorize just complaint. Foreign powers would use such breach of faith to deter their subjects from emigrating to the United

States. Mercer had the same idea. Baldwin still thought that discrimination as to birth was no more objectionable than that of age, in the propriety of which all had concurred. The vote resulted: ayes, 5 (Conn., N. J., Penn., Md., and Va.); noes, 6 (N. H., Mass., Del., N. C., S. C., Ga.). A motion to insert five years for seven was lost by a vote of 3 to 7. The principle involved was that of greater privileges to foreigners, and the vote was as the preceding one, except that New Jersey now went with the majority and Pennsylvania divided. The section was then agreed to unanimously as amended, and had attained its final form.[6]

I return now to consider the term of citizenship to be required of a senator. This was four years in the report of the Committee of Detail. Gouverneur Morris moved to change to fourteen years, and urged the danger of admitting strangers to the public councils. Pinckney seconded the amendment and urged the treaty power of the Senate against a short term qualification. There was peculiar danger and impropriety in opening the Senate's door to those who had foreign attachments. Mason highly approved the policy of the motion. Except for the revolution-

Elliott's Debates, I, 240; *Madison Papers*, III, 1299-1302.

ary deeds of many, he would favor limiting
eligibility to the Senate to natives.

Ellsworth opposed thus discouraging meritorious aliens from emigrating to this country.
Madison could never agree to the proposed
amendment. He was not averse to some restrictions on this subject, but any restriction
in the Constitution was unnecessary and improper. It was unnecessary because Congress was to regulate naturalization and
could require different periods of residence
for the different privileges of citizenship. It
was improper because it would give a tincture
of illiberality to the Constitution; because it
would prevent Congress, even by special acts,
from conferring the full rank of citizens on
meritorious strangers; and would discourage
the most desirable class of people from emigrating to the United States. With a stable
and reputable government established, great
numbers of respectable, liberty-loving Europeans would be ready to transfer their fortunes hither. Such persons, though not
coveting public honors, would be mortified
by incapacity. He did not apprehend that
the state legislatures, even if left at liberty to
do so, would choose any dangerous number
of strangers; nor that foreign powers would
use strangers as instruments of their pur-

poses. Their bribes would be expended on men whose circumstances would rather stifle than excite jealousy and watchfulness.

Butler was decidedly opposed to admitting foreigners till after long residence. They brought foreign attachments and different ideas of government, and were in every point of view dangerous. He himself would have been improper in public life till long after coming here. Franklin was not opposed to a reasonable residence requirement, but would be very sorry to see anything like illiberality inserted in the Constitution. The people of Europe and many in England were our friends. Many strangers served us faithfully in war, while many natives fought against us. Foreigners in choosing this country and coming here gave a proof of attachment which ought to excite confidence and affection.

Randolph thought that it might be problematical whether emigrants were, on the whole, useful or not, but he could never agree to disable them from public honors for fourteen years. Many were here on the faith of invitations, and would be made hostile. He would go as far as seven years, but no farther. Wilson mentioned that some of the ideas advanced might exclude himself, although he

shared in making the Constitution. Legal
incapacity produced chagrin and mortifica-
tion, even when one did not desire office.

Gouverneur Morris closed the debate by
urging that they should govern themselves
by reason and not by feelings, and not be po-
lite at the expense of prudence. Foreigners
would enjoy great privileges without office.
He would not trust philosophical citizens of
the world. The men who could shake off attachments to their own country could never
love another. They had no means of know-
ing what legislatures would do. The vote on
his motion to insert "fourteen years" for "four
years" was: ayes, 4 (N. H., N. J., S. C., Ga.);
noes, 7 (Mass., Conn., Penn., Del., Md., Va., N.
C.). Votes on thirteen and ten years each resulted the same.

Franklin reminded the convention again
that omitting a restriction from the Constitution did not remove restrictions. Rutledge
said that surely a longer term of citizenship
was required for a seat in the Senate, with its
greater power, than for a seat in the House of
Representatives, where seven years had been
required. Williamson thought it more necessary to guard the Senate, as bribery and
cabal would be easier in the electing legislatures. Randolph would agree to nine years,

expecting a reduction to seven years, if a motion to reconsider the term for the House of Representatives should reduce it. Delaware and Virginia changed to the restrictive side, North Carolina divided, and the proposition for nine years carried 6 to 4. The section as amended was agreed to *nem. con.,* and passed through the later stages without change.[7]

Art. VII, sec. 1 of the report of the Committee of Detail contained the following:

The legislature of the United States shall have the power . . . . 3. To establish a uniform rule of naturalization throughout the United States.

Clauses 1-8 of this section passed in the affirmative. Madison reports that there was only one vote cast against clause 1, that clause 2 passed *nem. con.,* and that clauses 4, 5, and 6 were agreed to *nem. con.* Apparently clause 3 (as above) passed without important comment, and with slight, if any, opposition.[8] The Committee on Style changed "a uniform rule" to "an uniform rule," a change not approved today.[9]

The report under consideration contained no age or birth qualification for President. On September 4 a special Compromise Committee of one member from each state, to

7 *Elliott's Debates,* I, 235; *Madison Papers,* III, 1273-76.

8 *Elliott's Debates,* I, 245; *Madison Papers,* V, 434.

9 *Elliott's Debates,* I, 298; *Madison Papers,* III, 1549.

which had been referred parts postponed or passed by, reported:

Sec. 2. No person except a natural-born citizen, or a citizen of the United States at the time of the adoption of the Constitution, shall be eligible to the office of President.

This was agreed to *nem. con.,* and embodied in the final draft.[10]

The Committee of Detail, in defining the jurisdiction of the Supreme Court, extended it

to controversies . . . . between a state and citizens of another state; between citizens of different states; and between a state, or the citizens thereof, and foreign states, citizens, or subjects.[11]

Later it was made the judicial power that was to extend to these controversies. For the present purpose there is need only to notice the mention of state citizenship.

The Articles of Confederation had provided that

the free inhabitants of each of these States, paupers, vagabonds, and fugitives from justice excepted, shall be entitled to all privileges and immunities of free citizens in the several States, and the people of each State shall have free ingress and regress to and from any other State, and shall enjoy therein all the privileges of trade and commerce, subject to the same duties, impositions, and restrictions as the inhabitants thereof respectively.

The corresponding provision in the Constitution appears first in the draft of the Commit-

[10] *Elliott's Debates,* I, 283, 291; V, 522.   [11] *Ibid.,* I, 229.

tee of Detail, as follows: "The citizens of each State shall be entitled to all privileges and immunities of citizens in the several States." This was agreed to as reported, 9 to 1, South Carolina opposing and Georgia divided. There is no record of discussion upon it, and it remained unchanged in the final draft.[12]

About the close of the convention Hamilton gave to Madison a paper outlining the Constitution as he would have wished it to have been proposed. Representatives, except in the first instance, were to be chosen "by the free male citizens and inhabitants of the several States." "The citizens and inhabitants of the several States" having land were to choose electors, who should choose the senators. No person was to be eligible to the office of president unless already a citizen of one of the states or thereafter born a citizen of the United States. A senator or representative at the time of his election should be a citizen and an inhabitant of the state in which he was chosen. Finally, "the citizens of each State shall be entitled to the rights, privileges, and immunities of citizens in every other State." [13]

[12] *Op. cit.*, I, 229, 272; IV, 2.
[13] *Madison Papers*, III, Appendix, xvi.

CHAPTER III

THE ACT OF 1790

The Act of 1790 was the first response of Congress to the grant of power to pass a uniform rule of naturalization. More immediately it was a response to the following clause from Washington's annual message (January 8, 1790):

Various considerations also render it expedient that the terms on which foreigners may be admitted to the rights of citizens should be speedily ascertained by a uniform rule of naturalization.

The bill was reported by a special committee of three appointed on the recommendation of the House Committee of the Whole on the State of the Union, to prepare and bring in a bill or bills for establishing a uniform rule of naturalization.

While it was in preparation the House discussed at some length questions raised by a petition of one H. W. Dobbyn, of Ireland, praying Congress to grant him lands on terms to encourage him to bring settlers to this country. A committee had reported upon this petition in favor of empowering the secretary of the treasury to sell not less than fifty thousand acres in one tract. On the one hand, it was objected that Dobbyn was an alien and might not be able to conform to the new plan for naturalization soon to be reported; that both naturalization and land sales ought to be by general laws; and that, in view of the notoriously rapid growth of population from the present inhabitants, sufficient in itself to people the territory, it was a mistake to throw away lands on foreign speculators, who were less likely to harmonize with, than, if numerous, to embarrass, a republican government. It was replied that it was important to attend to the proposals of foreigners—especially of intending citizens—for the purchase of lands; and that the condition of complying with the laws might be inserted in the contract. The report was laid on the table.[1]

When the naturalization bill was reported, the House debated it at considerable length, recommitted it to a committee of ten, which reported an amendatory bill, and discussed the latter for several days. Various amendments were agreed to, and the bill passed. In the Senate there was preliminary consideration in committee of the whole, a favorable report from a special committee, and further consideration in committee of the

[1] *Annals of Congress,* First Congress, Second Session, 1097, 1104, 1108, 1110; January 20, 1790.

whole on five successive days. The bill then passed with an amendment, in which the House concurred at once.[2]

The debate in the lower house, before the bill was recommitted, is reported quite fully. Of the later debates in either house there is no record;[3] nor can the course of amendments be traced. The original bill provided that all free white persons who had already migrated into the United States, who should prove by oath that they intended to reside in the United States, take an oath of allegiance, and "shall have resided in the United States for one whole year,"should be entitled to all the rights of citizenship, except that of holding office under either a state or the general government. For office-holding a residence of two years longer was required.[4]

Nineteen members are known to have participated in the first debate, upon a motion of Tucker (S. C.) to strike out the requirement of one year's residence for landholding. Six of them spoke three times, and seven others twice. The radical nature of the proposition to require no previous residence for ad-

---

[2] *House Journal*, First Congress, Second Session, 146, 147, 159, etc.; *Senate Journal*, 1, 34-48; *Annals of Congress*, First Congress, Second Session, 988, 989, 992, etc.; 1094, 1095, 1147, 1460, 1463, 1516.

[3] Except for Maclay's account of what occurred in the Senate.

[4] *Annals of Congress*, First Congress, Second Session, 1147.

mission to citizenship, except for office-holding, doubtless gave a special color to the various expressions of opinion, and makes some of them seem more conservative than they otherwise would have been.

The main lines of argument may be exhibited under a few general heads, such as constitutional and legal questions, protection from dangers, and the promotion of immigration. The constitutional questions were two. One man (Jackson, Ga.) would found our law on principles of progressive and probational naturalization, and cited English law in support of his position. Another (Smith, S. C.) also insisted that a uniform rule might be progressive. Madison thought it a nice question how far they should admit to citizenship step by step, and Boudinot (N. J.) asserted that citizenship ought to carry with it full and complete, not partial, rights.

The serious obstacle in the way of progressive naturalization was the view of the sphere of national control that seemed to be involved in it. According to Lawrence (N. Y.), while Congress would establish the rule of naturalization, the effects of it were to be determined by the states. Congress had only to point out the mode for becoming citizens. The Constitution had fixed a term of residence for a seat

in Congress. It was doubly doubtful as to
the power of Congress to fix any such term
as a qualification for membership in the state
legislatures. Nor could Congress lengthen
the six-months' period required by New York
law for voting for members of the state legislature, to one year after citizenship had been
gained.

Huntington (Conn.) wished to leave the
naturalization of foreigners to the state legislatures. Stone (Md.) remembered that the
states withheld privileges even from natives.
White (Va.) ventured to doubt the power
of Congress to decide when aliens could hold
lands within the states. Seney (Va.) declared
that Congress could fix a long term of residence as preliminary to office-holding under
the United States, but could neither lengthen
nor shorten the term required by the states.
Again, he asserted that Congress had nothing
to do with prescribing the qualifications for
state offices. Smith (S. C.) stood alone in asserting that a uniform rule of naturalization
would make a uniform rule of citizenship for
the whole continent, and decide the rights of
foreigners generally. Tucker (S. C.) cited
the constitutional provision as to voters as
proof that the states and not Congress were
to define the privileges under naturalization.

Throughout the debate the principal rights involved in citizenship were regarded as land-holding and office-holding. Only occasionally did suffrage as an independent right receive notice.

Apart from the constitutional questions considered above, every point had to be considered with reference to its effect on immigration. The problem was to adjust the naturalization law so as to gain the maximum advantage from immigration with the least harm or danger to republican government and institutions, and to the other interests of the country. Page (Va.) held that European policy did not apply here, and that a more liberal system was permissible. It was inconsistent with the claim of an asylum to make hard terms. These would exclude the good and not the bad. He would welcome all kinds of emigrants; all would be good citizens. Lawrence (N. Y.) declared that they were seeking to encourage emigration, but that the term of residence in the bill would tend to restrain it. The newcomer ought to vote as soon as he was taxed. He was not likely to leave the country after taking oath that he intended to reside in the United States. All comers, rich and poor, would add to the wealth or strength of the country. The evil

to result from restraining immigration was
greater than the benefits from a term of residence. Conduct could be restrained by laws.
Smith (S. C.) urged that the intention of the
motion they were considering was to permit
land purchase and holding. Clymer (Pa.)
would admit to citizenship gradually, and
suggested that it might be well to admit persons to hold land without ever coming to the
United States, as Pennsylvania had done. It
would result in easy borrowing.

On the other hand, the dangers to be apprehended from foreign-born citizens who might
be lacking in character, in knowledge of, and
attachment to, free institutions, or in a stead-
fast purpose to reside in the United States, or
who might be paupers or even criminals, were
strongly urged by a majority of the speakers.
Roger Sherman (Conn.) presumed that the intention of the constitutional provision was to
prevent states from forcing undesirable persons upon other states. It was to guard
against an improper mode of naturalization,
rather than to provide easier terms. Congress
would not compel a state to receive emigrants
likely to become chargeable. It would be
necessary to add a clause to provide for such.
Hartley (Pa.) opposed admission to all of the
privileges of a citizen without a residence re-

quirement. To have such a requirement was the practice of almost every state. All modern experience had shown the propriety of a line between the citizen and the alien. It would not be so bad if only landholding were involved, but voting was involved. Even if the foreigner was qualified to vote, there could be no hold on his attachment to the government, and hence no assurance of a good citizen, without requiring a term of residence in which he might come to esteem the government. Madison believed it necessary to guard against abuses. They should induce the worthy of mankind to come, the object being to increase the wealth and strength of the country. Those who would weaken it were not wanted. If only an oath was required, aliens might evade the laws intended to encourage the trade of citizens, and thus have in trade all the advantages both of citizens and of aliens. It was a simple question that was before them—whether residence was a proper quality. He had no doubt that it was.

Jackson (Ga.) wanted the term "citizen" to be venerated. He favored a term of probation, and testimonials at the end of it, and would have the grand jury or the district courts decide as to the character. Sylvester

(N. Y.) also favored a term of probation and vouchers for good behavior. He suggested lodging the whole power of admitting foreigners in district judges. Page objected that Jackson's plan involved inquisition and expelling the unworthy. It led to a test of the faith and politics of all who came for admission. Every man taking the oath of allegiance and purposing residence ought to be admitted to buy land. He did not object to a residence qualification for voting. Stone (Md.) would give property rights after six months' residence, requiring an oath of allegiance and of intended residence. For voting and office-holding he would require seven years' residence, following the example of the Constitution in this respect.[5] An emigrant desired property and not political rights. Before he was granted the latter, he must have time in which to come to know the government, to admit the truth of its principles, and to have acquired a taste for this kind of government. Burke (S. C.) said that one year was too short a residence requirement, and seven years were too long. The time ought to be two, three, or four years. Sedgwick (Mass.) opposed admitting the outcasts of Europe. There was no necessity of peopling the United States

[5] *Pennsylvania Packet,* February 11, 1790.

thus. He favored guarded admission and a term of probation.

Boudinot (N. J.) opposed the amendment. He would rather increase the term of residence to two years, and omit the office-holding restriction. One speaker proposed that, if the residence requirement was omitted, a clause be added to deprive of their citizenship those who left the country and remained abroad a given time. Otherwise merchants and sea captains would evade the payment of duties by merely taking an oath of intent to reside in the United States. Another thought the mode of the bill was much too easy. Various states, and Great Britain in particular, required a special act of the legislature to naturalize. He wished to amend to leave naturalization to the state legislatures. One member proposed to receive farmers, manufacturers, and mechanics on liberal terms, but to exclude merchants and factors, and also criminals. Other propositions were to invalidate land titles, if residence was interrupted within three years; to grant inheritance rights in the United States only when the favor was reciprocated by European nations; to make easy the return of Tories to citizenship; and to recommit the bill to provide for the case of children born abroad.

Sedgwick saw no extrication from a wilderness of ideas more various than on any other question. The committee rose, and the House recommitted the bill to a special committee of ten members.[6] Its later course has been given in outline.

Maclay in his *Journal* commented upon the proceedings in the Senate each day that the bill was before it, and must be quoted in detail. On March 8 he said: The naturalization bill was taken up. The debates were exceedingly lengthy, and a great number of amendments were moved. Morris [his colleague] stood by me in one to enable aliens to hold lands. I engaged warmly on every question. It is a vile bill, illiberal and void of philanthropy, and needed mending much. We complained [7] that such an ungenerous bill should be sent us—or at least I did. They answered, "You have little to do," and that they had sent us employment.

The following day he had to wrangle with the New England men alone on the naturalization bill till nearly one o'clock. Johnston (N. C.) took part in some degree with him. His success had been tolerable—but such shuffling and want of candor! He had cer-

⁶ *Annals of Congress,* First Congress, Second Session, 1147-61; *Pennsylvania Packet,* February 11, 1790.

⁷ To the Pennsylvania members of the House.

tainly gained greatly, though. They had failed twice the day before in the attempt to throw out the two-years'-residence requirement; and his amendments went to cure this defect with respect to holding lands. Many members then declared their dislike of the two years, and wished the bill committed for the purpose of having that part rejected. He had agreed, but they were very unlucky in the committee they got.

We Pennsylvanians act as if we believed that God made of one blood all the families of the earth; but the eastern people seem to think that he made none but New England folks.

It was strange that they were born under republican forms and were so contracted on the subject of general philanthropy. Pennsylvania was used to the reception and adoption of strangers, but there was no class of people that she received with such diffidence as the eastern people. They really had the worst characters of any people that offered themselves for citizens. Yet they were the ones who affected the greatest fear of being contaminated with foreign manners, customs, and vices. Perhaps they were justly fearful as to adopting any of the latter, for they certainly had enough already.

Three days later the committee had re-

ported, but far short of the points which he
wished established. There really seemed a
spirit of malevolence against Pennsylvania
in the business. She had been very liberal on
the subject of admitting strangers to citizenship; she had benefited and did still benefit by
it. Some characters seemed disposed to deprive them of those benefits. He had moved
a postponement of a day, which was easily
carried, that they might consider the amendment. Izard (S. C.) had snapped, ill-natured
as a cur, and said "No" alone.

Four more days of debate and part of another
followed. The same illiberality still possessed
the New England men. "Immigration is a
source of population to us and they wish to
deprive us of it." Maclay was dissatisfied
with the work of his colleague, Morris.
King (N. Y.) was as much against them as
any, but he did it in an indirect way. Again:

All our old arguments went over and over again.
The fact is, the adoption of strangers has set Pennsylvania far ahead of her sister states. They are spiteful and
envious, and wish to deprive her of this source of population; but it will scarcely do to avow openly such ungenerous conduct. It therefore must be done under various
pretenses and legal distinctions. Two years' residence was
insisted on in the bill. We cared not for this, but let the
stranger hold land the moment he comes, etc., etc. Two
law opinions were supported in the debates of the day:[8]

[8] March 17.

one that the power of holding lands was a feature of naturalization; that lands, etc., could not be held without it. This doctrine was pushed so far by Ellsworth [Conn.] as to declare that the rights of electors, being elected, etc., should attend and be described in the act of naturalization. All that could be said would not support this doctrine. Ellsworth was even so absurd as to suppose, if a man acquired the right of suffrage in one state, he had it in all, etc. This doctrine it was seen would not carry, and now one more conformable to the common law was set up.

It was alleged that the disability of an alien to hold lands arose from the common law, and was separable from the rights of naturalization, as in the case of denization in England, where the crown could confer the right of giving, receiving, and holding real property. When an alien, therefore, was enabled to hold real estate, it was in reality by repealing part of the common law with respect to him; not by giving a power, but taking away a disability. It, therefore, strictly speaking rested with the respective states whether they would repeal the common law with respect to aliens touching the point of holding property, and, being a pure state concern, had no occasion to be made any mention of in the naturalization act, but must remain to be settled by the different states by law, as well as the rights of election, etc. We of Pennsylvania contended hard to have a clause for empowering aliens to hold, etc. but the above reasoning prevailed, and we lost it.

After another day's debate, he continued:

From the most accurate observation I have been able to make the conduct of the members has been influenced by the following motives: as Pennsylvania is supposed likely to derive most benefit by migrations, the Eastern members are disposed to check it as much as they can. Jersey nearly indifferent; Delaware absolutely so; Maryland as

Jersey; Virginia unrepresented; North Carolina favorable; South Carolina and Georgia want people much but they fear the migrations, and will check them rather than run the chance of importing people who may be averse to slavery. Hence the bill passed the House [Senate] nearly as it came up from the representatives.

The governing ideas, however, seem to be the following: That the holding of property was separable from and not actually connected with naturalization; that laws and regulations relating to property, not being among the powers granted to Congress, remained with the different States. Therefore, Congress would be guilty of an assumption of power if they touched it; that the holding of property was a common law right, and the disability of aliens to hold property from that quarter. King [N. Y.], Patterson [N. J.], Bassett [Del.], Read [Del.], Henry [Md.], Johnston [N. C.], all finally settled in this way, Ellsworth dead against this; the holding property (real) a feature inseparable from naturalization, etc. Strong [Mass.] rather inclined to Ellsworth, Dr. Johnson [Conn.] said about as much on one side as on the other. Few, too, is said to be a lawyer; but, though he spoke a great deal, he did not seem to enter into the distinctions. For our parts we wished the naturalization bill to be in exact conformity as possible to the existing laws relating to aliens in Pennsylvania; and this, I am convinced, would have been the case had it not been for that low spirit which contaminates public characters as well as private life.

It appears that all over Europe where the civil law prevails, aliens hold property. It is the common law of England that deprives them of holding real estate. The common law has been received by us, and with it this consequence. However, since we cannot get the rights of property fully acknowledged, it is best that the naturalization bill say nothing about it.[9]

[9] *Maclay's Journal*, 208-11, 213-17.

The new law provided for the naturalization of free white aliens after two years' residence in the United States, upon application to any common law court of record in the state where they had resided for one year. They were to satisfy the court of their good character, and take an oath administered by the court to support the Constitution of the United States. Minor children resident in the United States at the time became citizens of the United States also. Children born abroad of citizens were to be natural-born citizens of the United States, unless the father had never resided in the United States. Any citizen already proscribed by a state was not to be readmitted to citizenship except by the act of the legislature of the proscribing state.

CHAPTER IV

THE ACT OF 1795

At the beginning of the session of 1794-95, a House committee [1] prepared a bill to amend the act of 1790. The measure, reported by Madison as chairman, was debated at length,[2] variously amended, and, by recommittal, lost its original character as an amendment to the act of 1790, and became a substitute for it. Further debate [3] and several amendments prepared it for the Senate.

No adequate conception of the original bill can be gained from the published records. Dexter (Mass.) introduced the debate in committee of the whole. He earnestly called attention to the importance and necessity of amending the existing law. He described the present easy access to citizenship as dangerous and insufficient to prevent improper persons from being incorporated with the American people. Longer time was absolutely necessary in which to detect persons lacking natural attachment for, and prepossessed

[1] Madison, Dexter, Cairnes; appointed December 8, reported December 15.

[2] On December 22, 26, 29, 30, 31; January 1 and 2.

[3] On January 6, 7, and 8.

against, the United States. The importance
of the general subject was emphasized by
declarations that America was the last and
only asylum for vagabonds and fugitives, and
that the establishment of uniform rules of
naturalization was one of the grand objects of
the Constitution. His motion to strike out
the two-years'-residence requirement, leaving
the blank to be filled later, was supported by
forty-five members.

Dexter, continuing, referred to the facility
with which foreign agents could take the oath
in order to save tonnage charges. He proposed an amendment to remedy this evil, and
a proviso that those who renounced all foreign
allegiance forever, and declared on oath their
intention of becoming citizens, should pay no
more tonnage dues than they would if fully
naturalized. Giles opposed favors to mercantile people, since they were the least of any
attached to the country. Dexter thought
some of them brought large capital. Madison
said that the clause belonged to the commercial regulations, not here; and the motion was
withdrawn.

Giles proposed that a special law of the
state abandoned be required to reinstate persons expatriating themselves. Tracy (Conn.)
did not favor perpetual allegiance; neverthe-

less, he thought it ill policy to admit a man back after he had expatriated himself, when he must have lost real attachment to any government. The amendment proposed, even if proper, made return too easy. He suggested that a law of the United States, evidently a private bill for each case, be required also. To this Giles agreed. However, further discussion showed legal and constitutional difficulties in the way of such a course, and this amendment was withdrawn. Certainly it conflicted with the constitutional requirement of uniformity in the naturalization law. It is important to note the very general assumption that attachment to one or another kind of government was what determined men's migrations from country to country. This idea was so prominent that the element of fact represented by it must have been considerable, and the fact has an important bearing upon the question of the character of the emigrants generally.

The bill did not yet meet the approval of Dexter. He moved that no alien be admitted except on the oath of two creditable witnesses, certifying that in their opinion he was of good moral character and attached to the welfare of the country. His colleague, Sedgwick, supported him. The present time of European war was inauspicious for the indiscriminate admission of aliens. He had always opposed the government policy. Republican character was hard to form. Greece, Rome, and the Swiss jealously guarded their citizenship. They should take warning also from Saxon, Danish, and Norman England, and not invite or bribe the undesirable. America should husband its wealth in land, for many would be dependent when it was gone. The two amendments proposed [4] would check the number of emigrants and not exclude the worthy.[5]

Giles [6] wished to amend by substituting for "attached to the welfare of this country," in Dexter's amendment, "attached to a Republican form of government." Dexter preferred "attached to the constitution of the United States." Giles had little or no objection, but soon after had the amendment changed to "attached to the principles of the government of the United States." In the final form "government" is changed to "constitution," and the phrase reads, "attached to the principles of the constitution of the United States."

W. J. Dayton would want a court to determine the nature of evidence submitted.

[4] Requiring longer residence and evidence of character.
[5] The end of the first day's debate.   [6] December 26.

Poor men were more desirable than merchants, and it would be hard for them to get
two witnesses. Madison agreed that it would
perhaps be difficult for many citizens, who
might have moved about, to find two reputable witnesses who could swear to the purity
of their principles for three years back.[7]   He
objected to requiring men to swear that they
preferred the Constitution.   They might be
honest in determining to support the government, and yet think some other form better.
Dexter, in reply, mentioned the abuses that
had happened in the present form of admitting citizens, and said that the poor, if
deserving, could get proofs as easy as the
rich.   Murray (Md.) was indifferent if not
fifty emigrants came to the continent in a
year.   It was unjust to hinder, but impolitic
to encourage, them.   They might contami-
nate. The amendment requiring two witnesses as to the moral character and political
opinions of candidates for naturalization then
passed.

On the 29th an effort to strike out "moral"
from the phrase "good moral character" in
the amendment was successfully opposed, on
the grounds that the word had nothing to do

[7] The reference to three years at this time is inexplicable. The
time between declaration of intention and admission must have been
fixed before the five years' residence period was determined.

with religion, and that to omit it would slander the American character.

Mr. Sedgwick desired to give property rights without suffrage, but did not know whether the Constitution authorized it or not. This raised again in the House the old question which, according to *Maclay's Journal*,[8] was settled in the Senate during the debate of 1790, in strict accordance with modern ideas; but there is no report of further discussion upon it. The clause last considered passed, and the discussion recurred to a question presented by Giles and Tracy in the debate of the first day. A motion by Giles had been withdrawn, but it now appeared as the third resolution in the report under consideration,[9] as follows: That an American citizen who had expatriated himself should not be restored to citizenship, without a special act of Congress and of the state that he had abandoned. Madison did not think that Congress by the Constitution had any authority to readmit American citizens. It was granted to them to admit only aliens. Sedgwick was very willing that they should never be readmitted.

A motion by Hillhouse (Conn.),[10] that if

8 See p. 47.

9 Probably this was the report in preparation by the committee of the whole.

10 December 30.

any American citizen should thereafter become a citizen of a foreign state, he should
not be again admitted, gave rise to more than
three hours of debate. Dunlap's American
Daily Advertiser says that it was in various
shapes and difficult to summarize.[11] The *Annals* report the ideas of two speakers only.
Murray (Md.) hoped the motion would suc-
ceed. It was unnecesary to decide whether
men could expatriate themselves without the
express consent of their country. He thought
they could. The United States practice
favored this view, for a government's acceptance of allegiance presupposed the right to
tender it. But there was little danger of
worthy citizens throwing off their allegiance;
and, in any case, prohibiting a return would be
a sufficient penalty. On the other hand, Baldwin (Ga.) expressed the strongest disapproval of the idea of expatriating all persons
who became citizens of another country.
Many were made such merely as a mark of
esteem, and had no design of renouncing their
allegiance to the United States.[12] There is no
report of the action by which this motion
failed.

[11] January 5, 1799.

[12] In this connection an item from *The Life and Letters of
Joel Barlow,* by C. B. Todd, (p. 97), is of interest. It refers to
a list of seven "Anglais" in *The Patriote* of September 25, 1792,

Debate recurred the following day upon the proposition to require both state and federal consent for repatriation. A motion by Smith (S. C.) to strike out this resolution, leaving the law as it stood, was rejected. It seemed thus in a fair way to become law, but did not appear again. Madison certainly opposed what he held to be unconstitutional, and probably his committee, when again in charge of the bill, dropped this superlatively patriotic proposition. In later years, however, the idea was revived several times, indicating the persistence of the thought that a man's change of country is due to choice of government, and that, therefore, one who has abandoned the United States has disapproved of its government, and, as a rule, cannot or will not adequately repent of this ill-doing.

After some discussion, Giles moved to require the renunciation in court of any titles of nobility. He thought this would be useful, if anything was to be done to prevent the im-

upon whom the French National Convention proposed to confer the title of "Citizen of France." Among them was Joel Barlow. It continues: "Save Washington and Hamilton, Barlow was the only American on whom the privileges of French citizenship had been conferred."

Moncure D. Conway, in the *Writings of Paine* (III, 97), states that on August 26, 1792, the National Assembly conferred the title of "French Citizens" on nineteen persons. Among them were Paine (spelled Payne), Washington, Hamilton, and Madison. The others include such names as Bentham, Wilberforce, Klopstock, Kosciusko, and Pestalozzi. Both Virginia and Maryland had naturalized La Fayette.

proper admixture of foreigners. Smith was entirely opposed to this. A similar attempt made in one of the state legislatures some years before was dropped as improper. The public mind was completely guarded against the introduction of titles, and they would never become current. Congress could not declare it a crime to call a man viscount. He doubted the constitutional right of the measure, for they had no authority to take away titles. Dexter was averse to titles, but did not like to make laws against them. Page (Va.) highly recommended the motion. Giles urged that there was no harm in expressing what Dexter had said was implied in the Constitution. The strange turn in affairs in Europe had not been foreseen, nor the resulting danger of an inundation of titled fugitives. Madison approved the motion. It was exactly the thing to exclude from citizenship those who would not renounce titles. The Revolution would infallibly have abolished any titles existing here. With opposition from both South Carolina and Massachusetts, and support reported only from his own state, Giles thought it best to withdraw his motion temporarily.[13] Madison said that the thing most

[13] The bill with amendments was at this point in the debate reported from the committee of the whole to the House. Discussion was renewed there the following day (January 1, 1795), and the amendments reported were quickly agreed to.

to be feared was that alien immigrants should obtain property in American shipping. They could thus clandestinely favor particular nations in trade. He would require a longer time for gaining certain trade rights, if he made any distinctions in the law. Giles, by renewing the motion for the renouncing of titles,[14] then prolonged the debate for two days. His amendment was as follows:

And, in case any such alien applying for admission to become a citizen of the United States shall have borne any hereditary title, or been of any of the orders of nobility, in the Kingdom or State from which he came, in addition to the requisites of this and the fore-recited act, he shall make an express renunciation of his title or order of nobility, in the court to which his application shall be made, before he shall be entitled to such admission; which renunciation shall be recorded in the said court.

He declared that stronger evidence was necessary to make sure that all pretense of a title had been renounced. He had voted for clauses to guard against Jacobin extremes,[15] and would now guard against the more dangerous aristocrats, of whom it was highly probable they would soon have great numbers here. A large part of Europe had declared against titles, and there was no guess-

[14] It was first offered in committee of the whole, and now renewed in the House.

[15] This may refer to any of the more stringent provisions of the bill, and especially to the renunciation of allegiance and the evidence required of attachment to the United States.

ing where the process would stop. The French
nobility numbered twenty thousand, a great
proportion of whom might finally be expected here. This fugitive nobility might acquire
influence here, and there was no law to prevent them from voting or coming to Congress.[16] Dexter said that he was not very
anxious about it, but opposed the amendment.
Priestcraft had done more mischief than aris-
tocracy.

Madison took middle ground as to the importance of the question; apparently he had
moderated his views somewhat since he had
last spoken upon it. Republicanism, he
thought, was likely to pervade Europe generally, and it was hard to guess how many
titled characters might be thrown out. It was
reasonable that crowds of them coming here
should be required to renounce everything
contrary to the spirit of the Constitution.
Hereditary titles were proscribed by the Constitution. He would not wish to have a citizen
who refused the proposed oath. Page (Va.)
believed the class principle would come in and
produce mischievous effects here as elsewhere. He did not want to see a duke contest an election to Congress with a citizen.

[16] Giles must here be taken to mean that a naturalized foreigner might vote, and that one who had been seven years a citizen of the United States might be sent to Congress.

Sedgwick declared that, in taking the oath of allegiance, nobility was solemnly abjured, for that oath destroyed all connection with the old government. To his, "Why reprovide?" Giles retorted, "Why not provide for it directly, if implied?" and declared that he should call for the yeas and nays on his motion. Nicholas (Va.) was sure that they ought to require an oath that the new citizen would never accept any title.

Lee (Va.) was sorry they had so long agitated an unimportant matter. In the minds of some, the motion was characterized by frivolity and inefficiency. He saw no shadow of foundation to build alarm upon. One might in this free country call himself by any name or title. Not titles but privileges were the dangerous thing. By the equal division of estates here, individuals were prevented from being [17] so rich as to trample upon the necks of their equals. Personally, he was very indifferent in the matter; but as tending to spread a false alarm, it was his duty to oppose the motion. Scott (Pa.) was for the motion on the ground that, it being unlawful to manufacture titles here, it was [18] unlawful to import them. If the importation was allowed, titles

[17] I. e., " becoming."
[18] Probably "should be."

would soon be as prevalent here as in England.

At this point Dexter announced that he would vote for Giles's amendment with a further amendment for renouncing slaves. He offered the following:

And, also, in case such alien shall, at the time of his application, hold any person in slavery, he shall in the same manner renounce all right and claim to hold such person in slavery.

Thatcher (Mass.) would add, "and that he never will possess slaves." Giles replied that he should think his amendment very important, if such extraordinary resources were adopted against it. He was sorry to see slavery made a jest, and it had no proper connection with the subject. He owned slaves, regretted it, and should rejoice to be shown the way out. The thing was reducing itself as fast as it was prudent. Why was such opposition as this made to the call for the yeas and nays. Madison declared that Virginia was reducing the number of her slaves. The motion would have a bad effect upon the minds of the slaves, or he might vote for it. Nicholas (Va.) said that Dexter had more than once hinted a view that a slave-owner was unfit for the legislature of a republican form of government; and retorted that he should know something of slavery. Dexter replied that the call for the yeas and nays was made with the design to hold up certain people to public odium. He would withdraw his amendment, if the Giles motion was withdrawn. Heath (Va.) said that the introduction of slavery was highly improper. The Constitution forbade any proposal to abolish it for years to come. The amendment was offered in the face of an express article of the Constitution. Sedgwick declared, with some warmth, that the design in the yeas and nays call was to fix upon members a stigma as friends of nobility, when they were not so. In this agitated state the House adjourned, but renewed the discussion the next day, and in committee of the whole.[19]

Bourne (R. I.)[20] was against both amendments. There were numerous checks against nobility in the Constitution. A man could renounce an hereditary title only for himself; his children would still inherit it. At this point Dexter withdrew his motion, in the hope that the yeas and nays would not be taken; and Giles then agreed to give up his part of the call. Hillhouse was convinced by reflection that the amendment would indirectly es-

[19] *Annals,* January 2, 1795, p. 1041.

[20] The debate does not show which Bourne this is, but the vote of the Rhode Island member was against both amendments.

tablish the principle that privileged orders
might exist among them, an idea that he rejected and reprobated.   Privileged orders
were merely local in privileges, yet this
motion tended to decide otherwise. He would
exclude titled foreigners from naturalization
to the extent of voting and office-holding.
Later he declared that he would support an
amendment to exclude all foreigners from any
office.   The present amendment, however,
was trifling and would make them ridiculous.
Wadsworth (Conn.) knew nothing so impossible as the establishment of an American
nobility, and the amendment was entirely useless.   Fisher Ames (Mass.) opposed giving
effect by law to chimerical whimsies, both
trifling and worthless.   Nothing was more
opposite to just principles than the extremes
of those principles.

Smith (Md.) said that the debate at first
bore a trifling appearance, but had called up
all the warmth of the House.   Gentlemen
from the eastern states slighted the amendment as unnecessary, but southern members
said that they had some reason to be appre-
hensive.   Why not yield to them in concilia-
tion?   Murray (Md.) saw only ghosts of nobility involved, yet favored the motion for his
colleague's reason.   Madison expected a

British revolution, and expected the British peerage to be thronging this country. He would sympathize with them, but not admit them to citizenship until they were constitutionally qualified. Giles, in replying to the opposition, said that it was admitted that the Constitution and the will of the people favored the amendment. Other speakers again called the proposition totally trifling legislation. Congress could not hinder the use of titles. The Constitution even permitted any non-office-holding citizen of the United States to receive a title from a foreign king. A naturalized alien could accept his title again an hour after his naturalization, in spite of any law of Congress.

The House at length became very impatient for the question, but discussion continued as to whether the call for the yeas and nays was still in force. Two motions were made for it. Sedgwick appealed to the members, and one of them was withdrawn. This dispute ended when Blount (N. C.) declared that the yeas and nays must and should be taken, and twenty-three members seconded his call. Dexter immediately renewed his anti-slave-holding amendment, and required a roll-call upon it. His motion was lost by 28 to 63, while that of Giles carried by 59 to 32.

Only five members voted for both amendments, and only nine voted against both. The
five were: from Massachusetts, 2; from Rhode
Island, Delaware, and Maryland, each 1. The
nine were: from Connecticut, 3; from Pennsylvania, 2; and 1 each from Rhode Island,
New Jersey, Virginia, and North Carolina.
Members who voted for renouncing slaves
were: from Massachusetts, 12; from New
York, 5; from Connecticut, 4; from Pennsylvania, 2; and 1 each from New Hampshire,
Rhode Island, New Jersey, Delaware, and
Maryland. Against renouncing slaves the vote
was: from Virginia, 19, from North Carolina,
9; from Pennsylvania, 8; from Maryland and
South Carolina, each 5; from New York, Connecticut, and New Hampshire, each 3; and 2
each from New Jersey, Vermont, Georgia, and
Kentucky. After this vote the bill was recommitted, and came back to the House as a
measure to supersede entirely the act of 1790.

The word "forever" was stricken from the
renouncing clause, and then the questions involved in filling the blanks were discussed at
some length.[21] The reports of this part of the
debate are very incomplete. Madison said
that there was danger of losing the bill altogether by mere waste of time, if they descend-

[21] January 6, 7, 8.

ed to discriminate all the qualities of a citizen. Both the ten years and the seven years that had been proposed for the first blank were "by much too long," and would oblige the friends of the bill to oppose it. Baldwin (Ga.) suggested that the Constitution qualified for a senator in nine years.[22] Fitzsimmons said that ten years were much too long, and would make aliens enemies to the government. Boudinot referred to the recent executive proclamation that the country was an asylum to the oppressed of all nations,[23] and thought it bad policy to admit them and then refuse them, for nine or ten years, the rights of citizens.

So far as the very incompletely reported debates show, defining naturalization by degrees met with no favor. There is also no suggestion that states could grant the right to hold real estate on their own terms, apart from naturalization.

The bill passed rapidly through the Senate.[24] There was debate on a motion to insert in the first section:

[22] In fact it was a citizen and not an alien that was thus qualified by the Constitution.

[23] A Thanksgiving proclamation of President Washington, issued during the debate on this bill (January 1, 1795), contained the following: "to beseech the Kind Author of these blessings....; to render this country more and more a safe and propitious asylum for the unfortunate of other countries."

[24] The three readings occurred on January 9, 14, and 15.

That no alien shall hereafter become a citizen of the United States, or any of them, except in the manner prescribed by this act.[25]

It was agreed, however, to insert the words "any of" after "citizen of" in the clause that as amended reads: "That any alien, being a free white person, may be admitted to become a citizen of any of the United States, on the following conditions;" and then, by a vote of 13 to 11, "and not otherwise" was added. On the last vote the yeas were: From New England, 7, and 1 each from New York, Pennsylvania, Maryland, North Carolina, South Carolina, and Kentucky; the nays: 2 each from Vermont and New Jersey, and 1 each from New Hampshire, New York, Maryland, Virginia, North Carolina, Georgia, and Kentucky. Apart from a rather strong favorable bias in New England, sectionalism scarcely appears in this vote. Thus the words "a citizen of the United States" disappeared from the bill. The idea that citizenship pertained to the individual states dominated the Senate. The new relation determined by naturalization was state citizenship. The power vested in Congress to establish a uniform rule of naturalization was the power of making state

[25] This motion was withdrawn for amendment the following day, after the failure of an effort to commit the bill and the amendment.

citizens from aliens. By the final phrase the
assertion is made that this power is an exclusive one. It can hardly be that the negative vote upon it represents only opposition
to this view. It is more likely that it com-
prises also some who deemed that the Constitution itself was sufficiently explicit in the
matter.

The question of extending the act to the
territories first appeared in connection with a
motion to provide for the naturalization of
aliens, dwelling in the territories southwest
and northwest of the Ohio, in the territorial
courts upon the same terms as elsewhere.
The bill and this motion were committed to
King (N. Y.), Tazewell (Va.), and Brown
(Ky.) for consideration and report. King
reported [26] two amendments, which were
adopted. One was a substitute for the first
paragraph of section 1, in which "may be admitted to become a citizen of the United
States, or any of them," replaced "may be admitted to become a citizen of any of the
United States." The other struck out "thereof" from section 2, where it read:

That any alien now residing within the limits and
under the jurisdiction of the United States, may be admitted
to become a citizen thereof, on his declaring . . . .

[26] January 22, 1795.

The necessary changes were made to give courts in the territories power to naturalize therein.[27]   A final proposition, lost, was to add a clause to the bill in effect that every person naturalized should, at the time of his naturalization, specify the names of his minor children resident in the United States; and that the clerk of the court should send a certificate of the naturalization, and a list of the children, to the secretary of state for record at the seat of the general government.

This proposition also included provision for a fee to the clerk of the court for each person naturalized.   On this day, January 26, 1795, the bill passed the Senate with amendments, which were at once agreed to by the House of Representatives.   It became a law three days later, with the title: "An act to establish an uniform rule of naturalization; and to repeal the act heretofore passed upon that subject."

The conditions of naturalization under the new law were:

[27] The provision for naturalization in the territories having disappeared after its reference to King's committee, it was moved to add at the end of the bill: "Be it further enacted, That the provisions contained in this act shall extend to the Northwestern and Southwestern Territories respectively."   After debate on two days (wholly unreported), it was agreed to amend this motion by a provision to insert the necessary phrases in sec. 1.   On a later day (January 26) this amended amendment was adopted as follows: "In line five, after 'the States' insert 'or of the Territories Northwest or South, of the river Ohio,'" and provision was made for inserting "or Territory" after "State" in line 11.

1. Three years before naturalization a declaration of intention must be sworn to in a state or federal court. This must cover two points—intention to become a citizen and intention to renounce all foreign allegiance.

2. At the time of applying for citizenship, the alien must declare on oath that he has resided five years in the United States (and one year in the state or territory), that he does renounce all foreign allegiance, and that he will support the Constitution of the United States.

3. The court must be satisfied of his residence, good moral character during the required five years, and that he has been for that time "attached to the principles of the Constitution of the United States, and well disposed to the good order and happiness of the same."

4. Any title or order of nobility must be renounced.

The bill made an exception in favor of aliens resident in the United States at the time of its passage. They were to be naturalized upon declaring two years' residence, and meeting the other requirements above. The provisions of the act of 1790 in regard to children and proscribed persons were reenacted. New points in the law were: longer residence and a preliminary declaration of intention, renunciation of former allegiance and of any title or order of nobility, more specific mention of the courts empowered to naturalize,[28] and proof of attachment to the Constitution and the country.   No requirement of the former law was omitted.

[28] The act of 1790 mentioned "any common law court of record in the state."   This act specified "the supreme, superior, district or circuit court of some one of the states or of the territories. . . . or a circuit or district court of the United States."

CHAPTER V

THE ACT OF 1798

During the special session of 1797 [1] Brooks
(N. Y.), in the House, expressed himself as
thinking that the naturalization law allowed
foreigners to become citizens too soon. His
motion for a committee to prepare a bill to
amend it was laid on the table.[2]

The inaugural address of President John
Adams approached this subject only in its
reference to dangers, if anything partial or
extraneous should infect the purity of elections.[3] His speech at the opening of Congress
in November contained no specific reference
to the matter. His biographer and grandson,
C. F. Adams, declares [4] that he certainly de-
clined to insert recommendations, to restrict
the rights of aliens and to restrict naturalization, that were submitted to him by his officers.[5] A part of the address, however, related to the protection of commerce and the
defense of the country; and it was referred by

[1] July 1.

[2] *Annals of Congress,* Fifth Congress, First Session, 421.

[3] *John Adams' Works,* IX, 108.

[4] *Life of John Adams,* II, 300.

[5] Presumably, members of his cabinet.

the House to a committee [6] to inquire and report concerning any expedient measures.[7]

Months passed without a report touching
aliens or naturalization. At length a member,
Coit (Conn.), said that from the present situation he apprehended that changes in the
naturalization law would be necessary. He
proposed a resolution that the above-mentioned committee be directed to inquire and
report whether it was not expedient to suspend or amend the act of 1795. Objection
was made to the form of his resolution, and it
lay on the table two days.[8] It passed then
with the wording changed to the "usual
form," so that it directed the committee "to inquire and report whether any, and what, alterations may be necessary" in the Naturalization Act of 1795. The same resolution also
instructed the same committee to consider
and report upon the expediency of establishing by law regulations respecting aliens arriving, or residing, within the United States.[9]

About two weeks later, Sewall, for the
committee, made a partial report, which was
referred to a Committee of the Whole House
on the State of the Union.[10] The committee

---

[6] Of seven members.

[7] *House Journal,* Fifth Congress, Second Session, 93.

[8] April 17-19.

[9] *House Journal,* Fifth Congress, Second Session, 266.

[10] *Ibid.,* 281.

declared that by the act of 1795 aliens were permitted to become citizens of the United States when there was not sufficient evidence of their attachment to the laws and welfare of the country to entitle them to such a privilege, and that a longer residence before their admission was essential. It was also of the opinion that some precautions against the promiscuous reception and residence of aliens, while always advisable, were then more apparently necessary and important, especially for securing and removing those who might be suspected of hostile intentions. Three resolutions were recommended, in substance as follows: (1) that provision ought to be made to prolong the residence to be proved by an alien before he should be admitted to become a citizen of the United States or of any state; (2) that provision ought to be made for a detailed report and registry of aliens in the United States; (3) that provision be made for securing or removing alien enemies, males of fourteen years, after proclamation by the president and time allowed for removal, excepting such as had a passport or a license to remain.[11]

These resolutions were reported from the committee of the whole with very slight

[11] *State Papers*, XX, 180.

amendment; the first and second were adopted, and the third was postponed in order that
amendments to it might be debated. The
committee that made the inquiry was then
ordered to bring in a bill, and on May 15,
Sewall presented a bill supplementary to and
to amend the act of 1795.[12] Three days later
the Alien Enemies' Bill was reported, and the
House, by a vote of 51 to 40, authorized the
president to raise a provisional army in preparation for the expected war with France.[13]
It is thus seen that the new Naturalization
Act was closely connected with the war measures of the Federalist party. The bill reported received several amendments in committee
of the whole, was further amended in the
House,[14] and passed on May 22. It returned
from the Senate, three weeks later, with
amendments which the House at once accepted;[15] and was signed by the president on
June 18, 1798.

The debate on the resolutions began with
the statement that five years of residence was
a much shorter period than France required;
and that the committee thought that at least
ten years should be required, but might leave

[12] *House Journal,* Fifth Congress, Second Session, 284, 285,
295.

[13] *Ibid.,* 301, 303.   [14] May 21; *ibid.,* 305.

[15] June 13, 1798; *ibid.,* 335, 337.

the time a blank in the bill. Harper (S. C.) referred to what he called the mistake that the country fell into, in forming its constitutions,[16] of admitting foreigners. It had been productive of very great evils, which he feared would greatly increase. It was proper, and the proper time, to declare that only birth should entitle a man to citizenship. The United States had had experience enough to cure it of its former folly of belief. He proposed, as an amendment to the first resolution,

that provision ought to be made by law for preventing any person becoming entitled to the rights of American citizenship except by birth.

This was declared to be a substitute and was ruled out of order.[17]

Otis (Mass.) moved that no person alien born and not then a citizen of the United States should thereafter be capable of holding any office under the United States. Harper moved to add, "or of voting at the election of any members of the Legislature of the United States, or of any State." This, he said, would permit aliens to gain property rights and residence, but not citizenship. He continued in a radical and at times sarcastic strain. He

[16] I. e., state and federal.

[17] *Annals of Congress,* Fifth Congress, Second Session, 1567.

would let the descendants of aliens, if born
here, have rights. If the native-born citizens
were not adequate to the duties of the government, they might invite foreigners to do
business for them. If they were adequate, he
could see no reason for admitting strangers
who could not have the same view of government as the native-born. He was convinced
that

it was an essential policy, which lay at the bottom of civil
society, that none but persons born in the country should
. . . . take part in the government.

To this there might be individual exceptions,
but the Congress must maintain the general
rule. They would better have adopted this
principle sooner; he hoped they would do it
then. Champlin (R. I.) suggested the introduction of the word "civil" before "officers"
in the amendment, so as not to exclude
foreigners from the military and naval service
as officers. Smith (S. C.) believed that the
first resolution was an ex post facto one, and
that it could not be intended to limit the rights
of persons who had been two or three years
in the United States under the five-year law.
Otis thought that the objections of Smith
were partly well founded, and he would avoid
them by providing for those that had declared

intentions of becoming citizens. He wished time to consider the matter further.

The *Annals* then state that Harper withdrew his amendment in order to examine the Constitution, "it being suggested that the constitution did not permit restraining states in the admission of citizens."[18] This, I think, must be accepted as having clear and positive reference to state, as distinct from United States, citizenship. The constitutional point raised was a difficult one, not easily met, at any rate, by the anti-federalist or state-rights interests. It cannot have been dependent upon the 1808 clause, unless it is maintained that "migration or importation" includes admission to citizenship. The objection that the power vested in Congress to establish a uniform rule of naturalization was not exclusive, seems, indeed, to have been made for a time; but it is almost unintelligible, and must have found its support chiefly in interest rather than in reason. At any rate, it can scarcely have counted for much with a man intent upon excluding foreigners from office. He would not want Pennsylvania, for example, to retain the power of making citizens of the United States. One, and only one, insuperable constitutional objection to "restraining states in the admis-

[18] *Op. cit.*, 1569; May 2, 1798.

sion of citizens" is readily found, and it adequately explains the allusion. It is "the Electors in each State shall have the Qualifications requisite for Electors in the most numerous Branch of the State Legislature."

The nearly inevitable conclusion from this was that the qualifications of voters in the various states were to differ, and were to be determined by each state for itself. All the existing facts in state governments favored this conclusion. Nothing could be opposed to it except the uniform rule of naturalization clause, or some implication in it; and the conception of two distinct citizenships, state and federal—a conception in fullest harmony with, and with the closest analogies to, many features of the dual government system—met any difficulty therein. Summing up, then, it seems that the Constitution not only did not prevent "restraining states in the admission" of federal citizens, but did itself restrain them; also, that it clearly implied that there was to be no "restraining states in the admission" of state citizens. The conclusion is that it was this latter fact that was brought out in the debate in the language reported.

Venable (Va.) called Otis's resolution a proposition to amend the Constitution. The latter had fixed the rights of citizens. Foreigners must be refused citizenship or admitted to all of citizens' rights. Congress had no power of saying that men entitled by the Constitution to hold office should not hold offices. Otis held that citizenship did not always include office-holding; that no alien was ever permitted to hold office in Great Britain.[19] Macon (N. C.) declared that a citizen must have the rights of citizenship, and might be elected or appointed to any office in spite of Congress. Congress could only keep him from becoming a citizen. Otis replied that Congress, having absolute power (it could exclude entirely by fixing a long term), had conditional power, which was a mere modification of the former. He opposed opening a door to the intrigues of other countries. Certain countries paid chief attention to influencing the internal affairs of countries they wished to dominate, and these might get persons into the government. America was now getting to be more important, and this was a reason for the exclusion sought. Yet

[19] 12 and 13 Wm. 3, ch. 2, provided that no person born out of the kingdom, except of English parents, though naturalized, should be capable of holding any office under the king or of receiving grants. By 1 Geo. 1 it was provided that there should be no future naturalization without a clause declaring such disability, and that no naturalization bill should be received without such a clause. The clause is, accordingly, found in all later acts on the subject before the Naturalization Act of 1870. See 13 Geo. 2, ch. 7, and 20 Geo. 2, ch. 44, which remained in force until 1870. (*English Statutes at Large*).

he would accept the plan for extending the
residence term. Sitgreaves (Pa.) desired to
attain the object sought, but would avoid constitutional embarrassment. The way to do
this was to extend the term of residence
to prevent aliens ever becoming citizens.
There was no doubt as to "member of Congress being an office."

Otis then withdrew his amendment, and
the three resolutions were agreed to by the
committee of the whole without a dissenting
voice. The House at once concurred in the
first and second resolutions, but discussed the
one that became the basis of the Alien Enemies' Act. The questions at issue were its
effect upon immigration and upon the country's institutions and independence.

McDowell (N. C.) said that some parts of
the country still wanted population, even if
others did not, and he did not wish to distress the minds of foreigners. Rutledge (S.
C.) asserted that the change proposed would
encourage immigration, by giving greater security of good government. Foreigners came
to America to live under good government.
The president should have the power to send
away any emissaries of a government even
if not at war with it.

Sitgreaves (Pa.) considered the proposed

law an essential feature of the system of defense. There was a cankerworm in the heart of the country, and no occasion for specific proof of it. The fact was well understood by every member of the House. France admitted no alien even to residence without a card of hospitality. The measure involved no danger to any persons that were well disposed.

Allen (Conn.) moved to amend in favor of giving the president power at any time to remove any alien, but soon after withdrew his amendment. He held that the citizens of several other countries were as dangerous as those of France, were equally hostile, were even more so. Recently there had been a vast number of naturalizations in Philadelphia to support a particular party in a particular election. French agents and diplomacy had overcome Venice, Switzerland, and Rome, when they were in a much less alarming situation than that of the United States.

Otis's amendment, withdrawn in committee, came up again in some unknown way, and was defeated by a vote of 55 to 27. Otis opposed, ineffectually, an effort to restrict the new power of the president to a state of declared war. He held that the measure was of no use, if not applicable to the existing state.

Considerable discussion followed, and **the**
question of a constitutional right to exclude
aliens not enemies before 1808 was raised.[20]
In the outcome the resolutions were all referred back to Sewall's committee, with instructions to report bills.[21]

The debate in the House on the naturalization bill was mostly on one day.[22] Sewall's
motion to fill the blank time between the
declaration of intention and naturalization
with five years carried, apparently without
discussion. He followed it with a motion to
fill the blank time of residence with fourteen
years. McDowell did not wish to discourage
immigration, and held it to be to their interest
to attach foreigners to the country. He would
not object to seven or nine years. The record
states that fourteen years carried by a vote
of 40 to 41.[23] Again, on Sewall's motion, **an**
amendment carried to the effect that no alien
be admitted to citizenship from a country at
war with the United States.

At this point Gallatin, the indomitable
leader of the opposition to the Federalists,

[20] *Annals of Congress*, Fifth Congress, Second Session, 1570 f.;
May 3, 1798.

[21] *House Journal*, Fifth Congress, Second Session, 285, 290.
The membership of the committee remained unchanged, except that
Brooks (N. Y.) replaced Livingston (N. Y.).

[22] May 21, 1798.

[23] *Annals of Congress*, Fifth Congress, Second Session, 1776.

who soon became so well hated by them that they aimed a constitutional amendment at him to exclude him from Congress, set himself earnestly to the task of protecting the interests of aliens that were already in the United States. He began by inquiring as to the retrospective effect of the proposed law. Three classes, he said, were to be affected by it. They were:

1. Aliens who were in the United States before the adoption of the Constitution, and not naturalized by any state law before the passage of the act of 1790.

2. All aliens who might have been naturalized under the act of 1790.

3. Those who had declared their intention to become citizens under the act of 1795.

He hoped that an exception would be made for all these. The law of 1795 had favored all aliens who were in the United States at the time of its passage.

Gallatin dwelt at some length upon the anomalous conditions and the misunderstandings that had grown out of the change from state to federal control of naturalization, and spoke of the difficulties in the way of many residents of frontier districts in complying with the naturalization requirements. These points were brought up in explanation of the

neglect of many aliens for a considerable time
to become citizens, and to show that such neglect could not properly be held to imply a disregard for the privilege of citizenship. He
said that there were "a great number" of persons in Pennsylvania who were not citizens of
the United States, but who, nevertheless, believed that they were citizens. He declared
that it was a common error in most of the
states that naturalization by a state since 1790
made the person a citizen of the United States.
The mayor of Philadelphia, he said, had admitted citizens under the state law until 1795,
and these had considered themselves to be citizens of the United States. This opinion, that
a state had a right to naturalize, although
based upon a construction that he had always
thought to be wrong, had until lately generally prevailed. In Philadelphia, at the late
election, respectable merchants, who had previously obtained American register for their
vessels on the presumption that they were
citizens of the United States, were refused
the suffrage. The same mistaken view as to
the status of those admitted to citizenship by
the states had prevailed in other parts of the
Union. He presumed that since 1795 nearly
all of those whose citizenship of the United
States could be questioned, and who are near

a court, had been naturalized under the federal act. People who were from two hundred to three hundred miles from a district court of the United States had not always had an opportunity to be naturalized,

especially on account of a construction of the Act of 1795, which had prevailed in some counties of Pennsylvania, and which made it doubtful whether any court in the State, out of the city [i. e., Philadelphia], could administer the oath of citizenship.

Now they had discovered that they were not citizens of the United States, and they had had no opportunity to become such since finding it out. He would give a limited period during which these might still have the benefit of the existing law.

Sewall defended the measure of his committee, a majority of which, he declared, thought that no exception should be made. He himself was decidedly opposed to any alteration. Those who had neglected their opportunities could place no high value upon citizenship. They could already hold lands, and, judging from the then distracted state of the country, it was not wise to make them eligible in five years to seats in the government. The United States had given unexampled liberty of citizenship, and it was then high time to remedy the resulting evils. The proposed regulations were shown to be necessary by the existing conditions, and created no disadvantage, for the persons affected had had little chance of becoming members of the government they had left. Their change in coming here had vastly improved their opportunities. There was no good, but much danger, in the proposed change.

Gallatin was unconvinced, and moved as an amendment, in accordance with the views that he had expressed, the following: that any alien, resident in the United States before the passage of the act of 1795, and any alien who had made the preliminary declaration required by that act, might be naturalized under its provisions.

Craik (Md.) would prevent any foreigner, coming thereafter, from ever becoming a citizen; yet he thought that retrospective action was unjust. His statements corroborated those of Gallatin as to the continued practice of state naturalization, and the existing uncertainties as to its effect. Many aliens, he said, were not naturalized under any law, while many others were naturalized under state laws. There was much doubt of the legality of the latter, though, he declared, in Maryland and Virginia "foreigners are still naturalized by the states."

Bayard (Del.) said that, as states allowed aliens to vote for both state and United States offices, the only privilege denied to them was "the capacity of becoming members of the Federal Government." It was sound policy to deny this for the future, even to aliens already in the United States. The naturalization laws were no compact, but mere favors. In reference to favoring persons already in the United States, he thought that as many Jacobins and vagabonds had come within the last two years as might come in ten years more. Macon (N. C.) said that those with particular ends to be served were in already, and he would have regard to the lack of opportunity and the ignorance of the others. Sewall asserted that the proposed amendment offered to all aliens in the United States the opportunity to make the required declaration before the law passed.

There was, as a matter of fact, just four weeks between the introduction of this amendment and the enactment of the law; and another month had then passed since the agitation of the matter of more stringent naturalization laws had begun in Congress. Either one or two months was doubtless a sufficient time for sending important public information to distant parts of the country.

Neither period, however, would have nearly
sufficed to apprise aliens generally, even in
the near-by states, that an important measure
seriously affecting their interests was pending in Congress. And much more than know-
ing that mere fact was essential for their taking even simple steps to ward off the dangers.
It is, I think, doubtful whether many aliens
outside of a few large cities would within the
given time, as matters then were, have felt
any particular stimulus from the proposed
legislation leading them to declare intention
of citizenship.

Returning to the argument made at the
time, Sitgreaves (Pa.) thought that a mere
matter of expediency was involved in the question at issue, and that the dangers existing
were too patent to admit of the amendment.
Claiborne said that his state (Tenn.) had been
represented in Congress only since the winter
before, and it was therefore not strange that
many did not know the law. They had no
post-road and no newspaper. It would be a
great injury to deprive them of their right.
They had fought and bled in the service of
the United States, and were as much wedded
to the government as were any people. J.
Williams (N. Y.) declared that, while aliens
might hold land "by the laws of several

states," they also were taxed and should be represented. The motion of Gallatin prevailed in the committee of the whole with 52 votes in its favor.

In the House Coit (Conn.) opposed favoring those who were in the United States before 1795, and had taken no steps to become citizens. His amendment was lost by 49 to 32 votes. Sitgreaves proposed to amend the amendment of Gallatin so as to give one year's time in which to act to those in the United States before 1795, and to allow to those having given notice by a declaration of intention four years from the time of the notice. An amendment to change one year to two years was lost by a vote of 31 to 39. One year then carried with 59 votes for it. Four years carried by a vote of 47 to 31.

Bayard (Del.) [24] sought to suspend the operation of the bill for a limited time, to avoid the danger at that time of too great restrictions in a new law, but failed on a point of order. The bill then went to the Senate, and the House turned its attention to the Alien Enemies' Bill.[25]

The Senate referred the naturalization bill [26] to a special committee,[27] and continued

[24] May 22, 1798.
[25] *House Journal*, Fifth Congress, Second Session, 306, 309.
[26] May 23, 1798.
[27] Bingham (Pa.), Stockton (N. J.), and Tazewell (Va.).

the consideration of its own "bill concerning
aliens," or the Alien Friends' Bill. Lawrence
moved to amend this by providing that it
should not be construed to affect any alien
who had come to the United States for the
purpose of becoming a citizen, had made the
required declaration, and had "renounced his
allegiance and fidelity" according to the act
of 1795; or may do so "within——days."
The clause allowing future declaration of intention was stricken out by a vote of 14 to 10.
The amendment carried, 20 to 4. Those opposed to it were Goodhue (Mass.), Lloyd
(Md.), Paine (Vt.), and Read (S. C.).[28]

The naturalization bill was reported with
amendments,[29] the nature of which is unknown. Presumably they were of minor importance. The Senate amended the bill in accordance with the report, and upon its third
reading Anderson (Tenn.), representing the
interests of the unsettled West, moved to
strike out fourteen and insert seven years as
the required residence term. The vote on
this proposition was: yeas, 10; nays, 11.[30] The

[28] *Annals of Congress*, Fifth Congress, Second Session, 567;
May 29, 1798.

[29] June 8.

[30] Yeas: Anderson (Tenn.), Bloodworth (N. C.), Brown (Ky.),
Foster (R. I.), Marshall (Ky.), Martin (N. C.), Mason (Va.),
Tattnall (Ga.), Tazewell (Va.); nays: Bingham (Pa.), Chipman
(Vt.), Goodhue (Mass.), Hillhouse (Conn.), Latimer (Del.), Law-
rence (N. Y.), Livermore (N. H.), Paine (Vt.), Read (S. C.),
Stockton (N. J.), Tracy (Conn.).

yeas were one each from Rhode Island, New York, Tennessee, and Georgia; and two each from Virginia, North Carolina, and Kentucky. Vermont and Connecticut each furnished two nays, and New Hampshire, Massachusetts, New York. New Jersey, Pennsylvania, Delaware, and South Carolina, each one. The vote of New York was divided. Those absent or not voting were the two senators from Maryland, and one each from New Hampshire, Massachusetts, Rhode Island, New Jersey, Pennsylvania, Delaware, Maryland, South Carolina, Georgia, and Tennessee. The affirmative vote, with the exception of the one vote from Rhode Island, was entirely from states having extensive frontier areas. The negative vote was chiefly from the older settled states.

The bill from the House, and as it was finally passed, contained in the first section the provision:

That no alien shall be admitted to become a citizen of the United States, or of any state, unless in the manner prescribed in the act.

After the failure of his amendment to reduce the residence requirement to seven years, Anderson offered another, apparently intended to remove from the bill recognition of federal citizenship, and to establish the view,

so prevalent later in the State Rights' party,
that only state citizenship had any real existence under the Constitution. He moved to
insert "any of the United States" in place of
"the United States, or of any state," in sec. 1
of the bill as above. The vote taken on striking out the phrase shows the same persons
voting as on the seven-year proposition.
Eight supported the change, and thirteen opposed it. The only changes from the previous
vote were that Foster, of Rhode Island, and
Martin, of North Carolina, went over to the
side of the majority. The bill passed, after
further unrecorded amendment, 13 to 8. The
thirteen were the same persons as opposed
the above amendment, and the eight were the
supporters of it. Every opposition vote on
the final passage of the bill was from a state
naturally desirous of immigration. The opposition to France that culminated with the X.
Y. Z. exposures carried a number of votes for
the measure, in spite of strong local interest in
favor of attracting immigration.[31]

Near the end of the year of special privilege
that the new law offered certain aliens, the
South Carolina Gazette announced[32] that it
was "very probable" that there were "many

[31] *Annals of Congress,* Fifth Congress, Second Session, 561-77;
May 22 to June 12.

[32] June 13, 1799.

persons in this state" who intended to become citizens of the United States, and informed any such who were in the United States before January 29, 1795, that they must apply before June 18, 1799—i. e., within the next five days—or they would be on the footing of new aliens, and would be required to give five years' notice and make proof of fourteen years' residence.

A few months later,[33] a House committee reported on the petition of certain aliens of Mount Pleasant, N. Y. These represented that they came into the United States before the passage of the act of 1798, and had omitted to make the declaration required to secure them admission under the act of 1795. They now requested the passage of an act securing to them the rights they would have had, had they made such declaration. The committee saw nothing warranting a deviation from the general rule. They believed the law of 1798 to be fair and just, and fourteen years not too long to conciliate the feelings of aliens to the manners, laws, and government of their new country. They thought that the attachment of a man to his native country would not be obliterated in five years so as to make it prudent to repose the confidence in him that

[33] March 4, 1800.

the government must place in its own citizens. Hence, they held, the prayer of the petitioners ought not to be granted.[34]

In the closing months of Adams' administration a resolution presented in the House resulted in the appointment [35] of a committee to inquire and report, by bill or otherwise, as to the expediency of amending the naturalization acts; to admit to the benefit of the act of 1795 all persons entitled to it before the passage of the later act and since resident in the United States; or to consider and report on the expediency of repealing the act of 1798. Another resolution, referred the same day to the same committee, directed inquiry as to the expediency of admitting aliens in the United States before January 29, 1795, and since resident therein, to become citizens. The first of these contemplated reviving the residence requirement of the act of 1795 for the benefit of a limited number of aliens, or of extending the provisions of that act to all aliens. The other resolution proposed to admit to citizenship upon special terms all such aliens as had been in the United States the specified time, about six years. A bill was reported [36] to extend the privileges of

[34] *American State Papers,* XX, 208, No. 125.

[35] January 30, 1801.

[36] February 6, 1801.

the former act to a limited class of aliens, but the session expired with it unconsidered. A petition for private naturalization, the first observed since 1790, was referred and neglected also.[37] The Federalist party record upon this subject ends here.

[37] *House Journal,* Sixth Congress, Second Session, 781, 788, 804.

CHAPTER VI

THE ACT OF 1802

Jefferson's message at the opening of Congress in December, 1801, contained the following passage:

I cannot omit recommending a revisal of the laws on the subject of naturalization. Considering the ordinary chances of human life, a denial of citizenship under a residence of fourteen years is a denial to a great proportion of those who ask it, and controls a policy pursued from their first settlement by many of these states, and still believed of consequence to their prosperity; and shall we refuse to the unhappy fugitives from distress that hospitality which the savages of the wilderness extended to our fathers arriving in this land? Shall oppressed humanity find no asylum on this globe? The constitution, indeed, has wisely provided that for admission to certain offices of important trust a residence shall be required sufficient to develop character and design. But might not the general character and capabilities of a citizen be safely communicated to every one manifesting a *bona fide* purpose of embarking his life and fortunes permanently with us, with restrictions, perhaps, to guard against the fraudulent usurpation of our flag, an abuse which brings so much embarrassment and loss on the genuine citizen and so much danger to the nation of being involved in war, that no endeavor should be spared to detect and suppress it.[1]

Vigorous and comprehensive attacks were made by the Federalist press upon the mes-

[1] *House Journal*, Seventh Congress, First Session, 11.

sage; but generally they are noticeable for the lack of any reference to the naturalization question. Neither the editorial review of the message in the *Washington Federalist*,[2] nor six articles upon it copied from the *Anti-Democrat,* mention it. To infer from these a lack of desire to defend the existing law seems justifiable.

However, Hamilton, in a series of eighteen articles upon the message, which he signed "Lucius Crassus," devoted two to naturalization and a consideration of Jefferson's consistency in regard to it.[3] He said:

The next most objectionable feature in the message, is the proposal to abolish all restrictions on naturalization, arising from a previous residence.

This, he continued, was at variance with the maxims of all commentators on popular government, and with Jefferson himself.

The notes on Virginia are in direct contradiction to the Message, and furnish us with strong reasons against the policy now recommended.

The passage from Jefferson's *Notes* (written in 1781) quoted by Hamilton is as follows:[4]

Here I will beg leave to propose a doubt. The present desire of America is to produce rapid population by as

[2] December 16, 1801.   [3] *Hamilton's Works,* VII, 236.
[4] *Jefferson's Writings,* III, 190.

great importation of foreigners as possible. But is this
founded in good policy?[5] The advantage proposed is the
multiplication of numbers. Now let us suppose (for
example only) that, in this state, we could double our
numbers in one year by the importation of foreigners; and
this is a greater accession than the most sanguine advocate
for emigration has a right to expect. Then I say, beginning
with a double stock, we shall attain any given degree of
population only twenty-seven years and three months
sooner than if we proceeded on our single stock. . . . .
But are there no inconveniences to be thrown into the scale
·against the advantages expected from a multiplication of
numbers by the importation of foreigners? It is for the
happiness of those united in society to harmonize as much
as possible in matters which they must of necessity transact
together. Civil government being the sole object of forming societies, its administration must be conducted by
common consent. Every species of government has its
specific principles. Ours perhaps are more peculiar than
those of any other in the universe. It is a composition of
the freest principles of the English constitution, with others
derived from natural right and from natural reason. To
these nothing can be more opposed than the maxims of
absolute monarchies. Yet from such we are to expect the
greatest number of emigrants. They will bring with them
the principles of the governments they leave, imbibed in
their early youth; or, if able to throw them off it will be in
exchange for an unbounded licentiousness, passing as is
usual, from one extreme to another. It would be a miracle
were they to stop precisely at the point of temperate liberty.
These principles, with their language, they will transmit to
their children. In proportion to their numbers, they will
share with us the legislation. They will infuse into it their

[5] Hamilton omits from this point to "But are there" below.

spirit, warp and bias its directions, and render it a heterogeneous, incoherent, distracted mass. I may appeal to experience, during the present contest, for a verification of these conjectures. But, if they be not certain in event, are they not possible, are they not probable? Is it not safer to wait with patience twenty-seven years and three months longer,[6] for the attainment of any degree of population desired or expected? May not our government be more homogeneous, more peaceable, more durable? Suppose twenty millions of Republican Americans thrown all of a sudden into France, what would be the condition of that kingdom? If it would be more turbulent, less happy, less strong, we may believe that the addition of half a million of foreigners to our present numbers would produce a similar effect here.

At this point Hamilton ended his quotation, stopping just before the most important sentence that Jefferson wrote. It reads:

If they come of themselves they are entitled to all the rights of citizenship; but I doubt the expediency of inviting them by extraordinary inducements.

Jefferson also added that he would not extend "these doubts" to the importation of useful artificers.

Spare no expense in obtaining them. They will after a while go to the plow and hoe; but in the meantime they will teach us something we do not know.

Hamilton continued that the impolicy of admitting foreigners to the suffrage immediately was an axiom. The United States had already felt the evils of incorporating large

[6] Hamilton omits the last six words.

numbers of foreigners. Classes and antipathies resulted. In the infancy of the country, with a boundless waste to people, "it was politic to give a facility to naturalization; but our situation is now changed," and the natural growth was sufficiently rapid. He did not mean

to contend for a total prohibition of the right of citizenship to strangers, nor even for the very long residence which is now a prerequisite to naturalization, and which of itself goes far toward a denial of that privilege. The present law was merely a temporary measure adopted under peculiar circumstances, and perhaps demanded a revision. But there is a wide difference between closing the door altogether and throwing it entirely open, between a postponement of fourteen years and an immediate admission to all the rights of citizenship. Some reasonable term ought to be allowed to enable aliens to get rid of foreign and acquire American attachments; to learn the principles and imbibe the spirit of our government; and to admit of a probability, at least, of their feeling a real interest in our affairs. A residence of not less than five years ought to be required. If the rights of naturalization may be communicated by parts, and it is not perceived why they may not be, those peculiar to the conducting of business and the acquisition of property, might with propriety be at once conferred, upon receiving proof by certain prescribed solemnities, of the intention of the candidates to become citizens, postponing all political privileges to the ultimate term. To admit foreigners indiscriminately to the rights of citizens, the moment they put foot in our country, as recommended in the message, would be nothing less than to admit the Grecian horse into the citadel of our liberty and sovereignty.

In considering the justice of Hamilton's criticism upon the position of Jefferson, we must first remember that the *Notes* relate to Virginia alone. Then the facts of a new government, greatly enlarged territory, and the lapse of twenty years at the time of the message are to be considered; also the different conditions affecting the production of a literary work and an important state paper. Consider also that in the *Notes* the subject in hand was emigration and increased population, and that Jefferson began with, "I will beg leave to propose a doubt," and ended with, "I doubt the expediency of inviting them by extraordinary inducements." Note carefully the restrictive effect of "expediency," "inviting," and "extraordinary inducements." Consider that he asserted the desirability of getting certain classes of foreign immigrants, and that he urged sparing no expense to secure them. Finally, connect the strong presentation of the dangers to be feared from foreigners with the sentence: "If they come they are entitled to all the rights of citizenship." Surely there is here no semblance of "closing the door altogether," nor shadow of excuse for anyone to represent that he "would have wholly excluded naturalization." [7]

[7] Jefferson mentioned naturalization in one other place in the *Notes on Virginia*. In giving a summary of the laws, he said: "A

When we turn from the *Notes on Virginia* to the message of 1801, it seems that the position of Jefferson in the latter has also been misrepresented. Hamilton reads in the message "the proposal to abolish all restrictions on naturalization, arising from a previous residence."

Jefferson certainly did not define himself so explicitly. He asserted the wisdom of the Constitution in requiring for certain offices a residence *sufficient to develop character and design* and then questioned whether the "general character and capabilities of a citizen" might not "be safely communicated to every one manifesting a *bona fide* purpose of embarking his life and fortunes permanently with us." Whether a term of residence should be an essential part of the mode of manifesting this *bona fide* purpose, and attesting its permanent quality, is a question that Jefferson left entirely open, unless it can be maintained that in adding "with restrictions, perhaps, to guard against the case of fraudulent use of the flag," he must be understood to imply that he would have no restrictions in other

foreigner of any nation not in open war with us, becomes naturalized by removing to the state to reside, and taking an oath of fidelity; and thereupon acquires every right of a native citizen: and citizens may divest themselves of that character by declaring by solemn deed, or in open court, that they mean to expatriate themselves, and no longer to be citizens of this state."

cases. It is possible so to understand him, but it is, I think, unquestionable that Jefferson did not seek to express himself clearly to that effect. The natural interpretation of his words does not find in them so extreme a thought. But if it be held that Jefferson did mean to recommend the naturalization of foreigners promptly upon their landing in America, I think that at least as good a case can be made out, from the evidence of the *Notes* in the sentence, "If they come of themselves they are entitled to all the rights of citizenship," that in 1781 he had already reached the same opinion.

Others followed Hamilton in alleging that Jefferson was inconsistent in 1801 with the views expressed in his Notes on Virginia. A series of three articles on the message, signed "Recantator," appeared while the act of 1802 was before Congress. The last of these is a diatribe charging Jefferson with dishonest change of opinion and with seeking the suffrage of alien fugitives.[8] J. C. Hamilton also, in his History of the Republic of the United States,[9] tells us that the early opinions of Jefferson would have wholly excluded naturalization; and again that Hamilton, replying to the message, quoted Jefferson's early opin-

[8] *Washington Federalist,* May 19, 1802.   [9] VII, 148, 529.

ions against the admission of foreigners to citizenship on any terms.

In connection with the first of these misrepresentations occurs also a strange use of material to save Hamilton from responsibility with his party for the Federalist mistakes of 1798. The son is discussing the Naturalization Act of 1798, and has declared that "Hamilton's view differed from his party." In proof of this he writes the unqualified "He said that," and follows it with details of Hamilton's opinions quoted from the reply to Jefferson's message as given above. Readers are thus compelled to suppose that these words represent Hamilton's expressed opinions or advice at the time of the passage of the act of 1798, before the election of 1800 could have influenced either his thought or his utterance of it. Hamilton had said in the same article: "The present law was merely a temporary measure adopted under peculiar circumstances, and perhaps demands revision." While it is true that temporary conditions led to the passage of the law referred to, there is no evidence that any of its supporters intended it to be "merely a temporary measure." On the contrary, most of them probably regarded it as a compromise measure that stopped short of what they desired.

The paragraph of Jefferson's message under consideration was referred to the Committee of the Whole House on the State of the Union, which reported a resolution "That the laws respecting naturalization ought to be revised and amended." [10] The House agreed to the resolution,[11] and a bill was soon brought in by a special committee appointed for the purpose.[12] The most complete statement of its contents and purposes as originally introduced has been found in the *Kentucky Palladium*. A general interest in the measure is apparent on the frontier that was lacking in the eastern cities.

The *Palladium* noted that a bill had been reported for revising and amending the laws on naturalization, and that it proposed several objects. The first of these was to repeal the act of 1798, passed when the United States were threatened with being involved in European war. Besides the fourteen-years-residence requirement, the alien

---

[10] December 14, 1801.   [11] December 15, 1801.

[12] January 26, 1802; *House Journal,* Seventh Congress, First Session, 17, 18, 70. The record upon this bill in both *Journals* and *Annals* is very meager. The *Kentucky Palladium* for January 8 and 15, 1802, adds some details. Mitchell, in committee of the whole on December 14, referred to his having presented two petitions from aliens, and offered the following: "Resolved, That the laws respecting naturalization ought to be revised." To this an amendment by Giles added "or amended." One member sought to secure instructions for the committee that they should prepare the bill, and another opposed reference to a committee on the ground that the bill to be proposed would affect every state in the Union. The reference was made by a vote of 29 to 42.

was also subjected to a variety of forms and penalties which have, since the passing of that act, been disregarded both by aliens themselves and by the magistrates of places in which they resided.

The second object was to recur to the act of 1795 which required five years' residence, and make that the rule governing admission. There was a proviso against admitting alien enemies, and against receiving the mere oath of any alien to prove the time of his own residence in the United States, compelling him to establish that point by other testimony. The third object was to cause aliens to register their names in the office of a clerk of some federal or state court, a certificate of this registration to be produced later as evidence of the time when the alien arrived in this country. This provision was to apply to all who arrived after June, 1798. A final object was to explain some doubts relative to proceedings under the naturalization laws, within the state of Pennsylvania.

There is no report of debate or of the nature of the several amendments made to this bill in the House. The *Annals*[13] mention "some time spent" upon it.[14] The vote by which it passed was 59 to 27.[15] In the Senate a part

[13] March 4, 1802.
[14] *House Journal*, Seventh Congress, First Session, 123, 127.
[15] *Ibid.*, 129.

of the amendments reported by a special committee were adopted, and the bill was then
recommitted.[16] Again the Senate accepted a
part of the amendments that were made, and
further amended it.[17] Newspaper reports indicate that the Senate amendments did not
alter "the principle of the original bill," and
that "they are principally confined to the re-
instatement of several of the provisions of the
act of 1795."[18]

The Senate also struck from the bill a
clause that limited to one year the operation
of the special proviso for aliens who were in
the United States before 1795; required of
them "due proof made to some one of the

[16] *Annals of Congress,* Seventh Congress, First Session, 198,
200, 204; March 12, 18, 25.

[17] *Ibid.,* 251; April 1, 1802.

[18] *Philadelphia Advertiser,* April 13 and 14, 1802. Various
considerations render it probable that the original bill had only
four sections, and in most respects was equivalent to the first
three sections of the law. The Senate combined secs. 1 and 2;
perhaps transferred the part that repealed the original acts to a
new sec. 5; and probably inserted sec. 4, relating to minor children
of naturalized persons, to children of citizens born abroad, and to
persons already proscribed by any state. Some of the considerations
in support of these conclusions may be mentioned. The House
recommitted the fourth section of the bill (*House Journal,* 123);
a Senate amendment to the last line of the original is found in
the final sec. 3 (*Annals of Congress,* Seventh Congress, First Session, 252; April 3); the *Kentucky Palladium's* summary contains
four parts, arranged in harmony with these views; sec. 4 of the act
is not referred to in the *Palladium's* summary of the bill as introduced, and its provisions, as we expect the Senate amendments
to be, are taken largely from the act of 1795 (*Philadelphia Advertiser, supra*). Finally, the House amended a section proposed to
be substituted by the Senate for secs. 1 and 2 of the original bill
(*House Journal,* Seventh Congress, First Session, 187).

courts," in place of "declaring on oath or affirmation" that they had fulfilled the other
residence requirements; and inserted "immediately preceding his application" to modify
the state residence required in the same proviso. It also changed the word "admitted"
to "naturalized" in the last clause of sec. 3.
By the first of these amendments it secured,
for those who had been in the United States
seven years, the opportunity, not merely
within a year, as the House had provided, but
at any future time, to become naturalized
without a previous declaration of intention.
The next amendment made this proviso consistent with the general provision as to proof
of residence. The third amendment required
a quality of residence of those having the benefit of this proviso that was not definitely stipulated for as to others. The final change substituted the most precise technical term for a
very loose general one.

The bill passed the Senate as amended, by
a vote of 18 to 8, and was further amended in
the House.[19] It became a law on April 14,
1802,[20] and remains the law in all of its general
features after the lapse of one hundred years.
Two months later the *Kentucky Palladium*[21]

[19] *House Journal*, Seventh Congress, First Session, 177, 187.
[20] *Ibid.*, 194.   [21] June 17, 1802.

quoted from the *National Intelligencer* the news that the revision had taken place, and the following comment:

> The justice due to a large number of people who emigrated under the faith of existing laws, and the policy of opening the wilderness and acquiring the arts and manufactures of Europe required this revision. It is only the revival of the Washington system.

During the winter of 1803 a number of petitions, chiefly from aliens in Pennsylvania, were received by Congress praying for a modification of the Naturalization Act. The first of these asked amendment as related to aliens who came to the United States to reside while the act of 1798 was in force. It was objected to on the ground that it was extremely disrespectful by reason of some severe comments on the Adams administration, and that the law had been amended in the interest of the petitioners at the last session of Congress. One speaker urged care lest they "uncitizenize" themselves by going too far. After discussion *pro* and *con,* reference was lost by a vote of 32 to 49.[22]

The following day another petition was read containing an argument for easy naturalization. Irish aliens had been invited by Con-

[22] *House Journal,* Seventh Congress, Second Session, 324; *Annals of Congress,* Seventh Congress, Second Session, 465; February 7, 1803.

gress. Two years' residence in Pennsylvania and some other states was to give citizenship. Encourage aliens and you will prosper. "Neglect us, we suffer, but you are not served." It concluded with a prayer that Congress would admit to citizenship those aliens that were shut out from it by default of three years' previous declaration of intention, and restore the two-years'-residence requirement of the first naturalization law. Again reference was refused by the more emphatic vote of 23 to 61.[23]

Soon, however, other petitions of a similar nature were referred to a special committee,[24] but not without question and explanation that the objectionable expressions of the former ones were not in these. The committee worked rapidly, got leave to report by bill, and did so in three days,[25] as follows: Any alien being free white, resident in the United States between June 14, 1802, and since, may be admitted to become a citizen of the United States, or any of them, without compliance with the first condition of the Naturalization Act [i. e., without making declaration of intention three years before admission].

There was vigorous opposition when the bill

[23] *Annals of Congress,* Seventh Congress, Second Session, 474, 480; February 8, 1803.

[24] *House Journal,* Seventh Congress, Second Session, 339, 345; April 14 and 16.

[25] April 17.

was put upon its passage. Goddard (Conn.) was surprised that this bill was pressed —there was so little time left; none were less entitled to the time of the House than these persons. The language of their petitions was at first so indecent that the House had refused to consider them. They were returned within two days with the same signatures and language, except that the objectionable passage had been omitted. Someone had remodeled them. Dana (Conn.) also objected to giving more attention to these aliens than to citizens. Smilie (Pa.) defended them. He quoted the objectionable paragraph and asserted its truth. In substance, it was that from 1798 to 1801 aliens attached to liberty were abused in the administrative papers; the president was notoriously hostile, and could banish them at pleasure; an alien resident could have no inducement to declare his intention to become a citizen, as he was thus placing himself on a list of proscriptions [calling the attention of a hostile administration to himself].

He continued by inquiring what harm there could be in admitting aliens after five years of residence, even if they had not made a declaration of intention at a time when fourteen years' residence was required. Duty to the aliens and to their own selves required their admission. Fears lest foreigners should destroy or injure their political system were ridiculous. Labor is of the last (i. e., greatest) importance in the middle states. The measure saves three years of residence to a class of aliens, who without it must reside here eight years before their naturalization. Davis (Ky.) urged the turbulent and factious tempers of aliens, and verily believed that in less than five years they would be obliged to re-enact fourteen years' residence. Was it right or constitutional to apply four rules to some aliens and three to others? Some of the opposition feared that perjury would result from the measure. Lieb (Pa.) stated that the petitions showed many persons to be affected. Was there any magic in a declaration of intention fitting aliens for citizenship? It was the existing law that made inequality; it required five years' residence for some and eight years for others, who came after 1798 and before 1802. Only four at most of the required fourteen years had passed for these, and nine were given before it became useful to declare intention. An earlier declaration was a risk, and exposed the alien to transportation. Both the spirit and the letter of the last law were in favor of the present bill.

Three votes were taken in disposing of the

measure. Postponement was refused by a vote of 40 to 42. Griswold moved to recommit, as it was too late to amend in the House. If the measure carried, he wished it to carry with it a provision for a declaration of intention one month or one year before admission. The purpose of a declaration was to let people observe the character and behavior of the prospective citizen. He wished the select committee, also, to investigate the charge of forgery in reconstructing certain of the petitions. Recommitment failed, 38 to 42. The bill was then rejected by a vote of 37 to 42.[26]

A petition of Baltimore aliens brought up the subject in the House early in the following session,[27] and a bill was soon reported.[28] It passed the House by a vote of 65 to 38, and became a law on March 26, 1804.[29] Section 1 was the same as the bill of the previous year,[30] except that the words "or any of them" were omitted after "may be admitted to become a citizen of the United States." They had been in all the previous acts, except that of 1790, and their omission here indicates the as-

[26] *Annals of Congress,* Seventh Congress, Second Session, 569-74; February 21, 1803.

[27] *House Journal,* Eighth Congress, First Session, 518; January 6, 1804.

[28] *Ibid.,* 545; January 20, 1804.

[29] *Ibid.,* 655, 690.

[30] See p. 111.

cendancy of a new conception of the relations between state and federal citizenship.

Section 2 provided that when any alien who had complied with the conditions in secs. 1 and 2 of the act of 1802 (i. e., had made a declaration of intention, had registered the date of his arrival, and had received a certificate thereof) died before he was actually naturalized, his widow and children should be considered to be citizens, and should be entitled to all the rights and privileges of citizens upon taking the oaths prescribed by law. The House and the Senate each made one change in the bill as reported. It is probable that one of them made the change mentioned in section 1, and that the other added sec. 2 to the bill. The latter section introduced a new principle into the legislation on the subject.

McMaster refers [31] to the Federalist opposition in 1807 to the naturalization laws, as causing trouble; and to their cry of repeal those laws, give up to England her subjects, and do not wage war for protection of British deserters. It was this opposition that led, in 1808, to an effort in Congress to enact that all citizens shall be considered such no longer than while they actually reside within the United States; and that,

[31] *History of the United States,* III, 255, 256. See IV, 389ff., for some instructive passages in regard to the immigration of this period.

also, if any citizen shall expatriate himself, he shall, *ipso facto,* be deemed an alien, and ever after be incapable of becoming a citizen.[32]

This bill was reported [33] by a committee appointed,[34] on the motion of Burwell (Va.), to inquire into the expediency of amending the act of 1802. It was twice read, and reached reference to the committee of the whole a month before the close of the session.

[32] *Annals of Congress,* Tenth Congress, First Session, 1871; March 26, 1808.

[33] March 26, 1808.

[34] Early in the following session (November 30, 1808) Burwell renewed his motion for a committee, and soon (December 17) reported a bill in the same form as before. He mentioned a modification of it, to which his committee had not agreed, that he intended to propose in committee of the whole. The bill, however, dropped from sight with its reference as before. *House Journal,* Tenth Congress, Second Session, 133, 247, 368, 395; 19 *Annals of Congress,* Tenth Congress, Second Session, 864; December 17, 1808.

CHAPTER VII

THE ACT OF 1813

Within ten days after the declaration of war with Great Britain, in 1812, a committee was appointed in the House to inquire into the expediency of admitting to citizenship such British aliens (now alien enemies, and incapable under existing laws) as had emigrated to the United States while they were alien friends.[1] The mover of the committee urged that the immediate attention of Congress was required, as the courts were prohibited from naturalizing persons whose probationary period was ended and of whom state laws required military service. The government was pledged to these; they were strongly attached to the United States, and there could be no danger from admitting them.[2] The committee promptly reported a bill authorizing the naturalization of such British alien enemies. An amendment was added limiting to the next six months the time in which application for the benefit of the proposed law, and declaration of intention, could be made. An amendment to exclude from its

[1] *House Journal*, Twelfth Congress, First Session, 401.

[2] *Annals of Congress*, Twelfth Congress, First Session, 1561.

privileges all aliens of five years' residence in the United States who had not already made legal declaration of intention to become citizens was lost. The bill passed the House, without division, the third day after its introduction. It went through the Senate in three days, without amendment, and passed by unanimous consent.[3] July 6, 1812, it was sent to President Madison.[4]

Just after the opening of the following session, in November, a message from the executive informed the houses that this bill had been "liable to abuse by aliens having no real purpose of effecting a naturalization," and that, as it came to him too late to be returned for their reconsideration, he had permitted it to fail of becoming a law. He recommended that "provision be now made in favor of aliens entitled to the contemplated benefit, under such regulations as will prevent advantage being taken of it for improper purposes."[5]

Niles Register, in noting the failure of this bill, said:

It is understood that some amendment to the bill in one or other house in the course of its progress rendered it objectionable in the view of the president.[6]

[3] *Op cit.,* 317.

[4] *House Journal,* Twelfth Congress, First Session, 403, 414, 421.

[5] *Ibid.,* Second Session, 554.

[6] *Niles Register,* II, 304; July 25, 1812.

It seems to have had but one amendment, as
given above; and that one brought the bill
more into line with the suggestion of the message than it was without it. In the course of
the debate on a subsequent bill, the ground of
the president's opposition was explained to be
that the bill contained no authorization for the
removal of alien enemies before their naturalization was completed.[7] Interest in this explanation is increased when we remember that
the president who wrote this veto message
wrote also the Virginia resolutions.

The committee of the House to which the
message was referred reported a new bill within two weeks.[8] It authorized the admission to
citizenship, in the manner prescribed by the
naturalization acts, of all persons resident in
the United States or the territories thereof on
June 1, 1812, notwithstanding anything growing out of the existing state of war, provided
that no alien enemy was to be admitted unless
he declared his intention and made the application required within nine months. Nothing
in the act was to be construed to prevent the
removal, according to law, of any alien enemy
before his naturalization was completed.[9]
Besides the addition of this last proviso, the

[7] *Annals of Congress,* Thirteenth Congress, First Session, 467.
[8] *House Journal,* Twelfth Congress, Second Session, 554.
[9] *Annals of Congress,* Twelfth Congress, Second Session, 153.

substantial changes from the former bill were two. The date at which residence must have been acquired was changed from June 18 (the opening of the war) to June 1; the time within which declaration of intention could be made was changed from six months to nine months. A varied experience met the bill in the House. The committee of the whole reported it without amendment. The House amended it by adding as sec. 2:

That every naturalized citizen of the United States or the territories thereof, shall forfeit such citizenship upon his voluntarily removing from and remaining out of the United States or the territories thereof, for and during the term of two years.[10]

This is probably the origin, or a very early prototype, of the similar two-year term in various later treaties. Apparently, the radical amendment the bill had now undergone destroyed the interest of its friends in it. A month passed by when, on motion of the father of the measure, Lacock (Penn.), it was recommitted to a committee of the whole for amendment. The recommendation of that body, that the new section providing for expatriation be struck out, carried in the House by a vote of 71 to 43.[11] Lacock made an effort

[10] Shown by *Annals of Congress,* Twelfth Congress, Second Session, 153, in connection with *House Journal,* Twelfth Congress, Second Session, 569 and 684.

[11] *House Journal,* Twelfth Congress, Second Session, 684.

now to amend by extending the naturalization of aliens to all those "who have heretofore, or may within nine months hereafter, declare their intention agreeably to law to become citizens of the United States." This amendment failed by three votes. It would have removed any question (such as arose with a later bill) as to a new declaration of intention being required from those who had taken the first steps toward citizenship. But much more important would have been the permission given to naturalize all alien enemies arriving in America within the next nine months.

A reason alleged by Bacon (Mass,), the following day, for opposing the bill, that it was impolitic to encourage the emigration of alien enemies during war [12] would seem to be valid only on the supposition that it was made at an earlier date, while the foregoing amendment was pending. But his motion to recommit to the committee of the whole for amendment, supported by Grundy, who wished to amend certain details of the bill, and carried by a large majority, leaves little possibility of doubt that he spoke at the later date.

For a third time the committee of the whole approved the bill in its original form, and it passed the House on February 23 as "an act

[12] *Annals of Congress,* Twelfth Congress, Second Session, 1076.

supplementary to the existing naturalization acts."[13] A day later the Senate special committee reported it with amendments. It was read the third time, as amended, by unanimous vote, and passed on March 3, entirely too late for further consideration in the House.[14] Just as the bill passed the House, a petition was received from certain naturalized citizens, formerly British, who, referring to a proclamation of the prince regent, declared that they were threatened by the English as traitors, if they aided the United States. They asked that the wisdom of Congress protect them.[15]

Third bill: A special session of Congress was held during the summer of 1813. Lacock, who had championed the cause of the enemy aliens in the House, had been transferred to the Senate. On the last day of May he presented therein a memorial of certain English aliens praying for admission to citizenship, notwithstanding the omission of certain forms of application. The language of this petition would seem to embrace the removal of the enemy disability, and also admission without

[13] *House Journal*, Twelfth Congress, Second Session, 689, 702, 703.

[14] *Annals of Congress*, Twelfth Congress, Second Session, 100, 102, 109, 121; *House Journal*, Twelfth Congress, Second Session, 736.

[15] *Annals of Congress*, Twelfth Congress, Second Session, 98; February 23, 1813.

a declaration of intention. In response to it, a bill was reported within two days, amended in committee of the whole in manner unknown and passed within a week of the receipt of the petition.[16] It authorized the admission, according to law, of all alien enemies who were resident in the United States at the beginning of the war; but limited to nine months the time for making the required declaration of intention. Nothing contained in it was to be construed to prevent "the apprehension and removal, agreeably to law, of any alien enemy, at any time previous to the actual naturalization of such alien."[17]

The bill met with no opposition in the House committee of the whole, but, when reported to the House, Burwell (Va.) stated that he wished to offer amendments, one of them being to confine the privileges of naturalized citizens to actual residence within the United States.[18] Later he waived his purpose to amend this bill, declaring that he should propose a radical change of the naturalization laws at the next session. He held it to be the duty of Congress to repeal its

[16] *Ibid.*, Thirteenth Congress, First Session, 19-23; May 31 to June 7.

[17] *House Journal,* Thirteenth Congress, First Session, 22; or *Annals of Congress,* Thirteenth Congress, First Session, 147.

[18] *Annals of Congress,* Thirteenth Congress, First Session, 147; June 9, 1813.

naturalization laws in *toto,* or to dry up the sources of collision with foreign powers arising out of them; but time was then lacking for mature consideration of the subject. He must oppose the present bill, unless it was amended, as it would give "to the numerous class of foreign merchants who have been ordered from the seaports, the advantage of availing themselves of all the benefits of citizenship, and the protection and privilege they convey, by merely declaring an intention to become citizens."[19] This objection involves the idea that protection would be given by the United States even to alien enemies who had taken but one step toward citizenship.[20]

Gaston (N. C.) had many objections to the bill. He secured a change in its wording to make clear that those who had already declared their intention should be exempt from a new declaration. A motion to validate any naturalization of alien enemies made since the war began was lost by a vote of 57 to 73. Further opposition arose to the bill in its existing form, and, with an amendment pending to confine its privileges to those who had already declared their intention to become citizens,

[19] *Op. cit.,* 154; June 11.

[20] It can hardly be that the privilege of the American flag in commerce is what is referred to. That would involve an idea about as unlikely and much more inadequate.

it was agreed *nem. con.* to refer it to the
Committee of Foreign Affairs.[21]   It returned
with three amendments, of which the House
accepted one, limiting the privileges of the
bill to aliens who had already declared their
intention, or of whom no declaration of intention was required.[22]   King (Mass.) failed in
an effort, probably in the interest of alien
sailors, to strike out the limitation to persons
"resident in the United States or the Territories thereof."[23]

Again those who wished to open the way
for the admission of all resident alien enemies
rallied their forces, and, by a very close vote,[24]
succeeded in recommitting the measure to a
favorable select committee.   Kennedy (N. C.)
supported their report at some length.   He
urged that the situation of the alien enemy
was extremely disagreeable, shut out as he
was from all mercantile business within forty
miles of tide water, and harassed by the adver-
tisements of United States marshals ordering
him to register.   The recent law relative to
seamen did not restrict their naturalization

[21] *Annals of Congress,* Thirteenth Congress, First Session, 154;
June 11, 1813.

[22] In the debate of the twelfth, Kennedy referred to a clause
limiting the privilege of naturalization under the act to aliens who
had declared their intention. This justifies the conclusion given as
to the nature of the amendment   (*Annals of Congress,* p. 433).

[23] *House Journal,* Thirteenth Congress, First Session, 74, 88.

[24] Fifty-seven to fifty-three.

until peace came. Those who thought that it did might amend this measure to naturalize only after five years' residence, and all difficulty would be removed. The measure would strengthen the country for war and relieve persons who had, for the most part, been banished by oppression, had fled to the only asylum open to them, and were now threatened again. In his section they were generally Irish. Some persons were contending for letting them be naturalized by state governments. In that case the United States could not claim them as citizens and screen them from punishment for treason. Could the government treat as alien enemies, and deny civil rights to, those who joined its armies? Such a course would sour the minds of those well affected. He had it on good authority that the president's opposition to the former bill was because it contained no provision for the removal of alien enemies previous to their naturalization.[25]

The House amended the report of the committee, evidently by reinserting the requirement of a declaration of intention before the outbreak of the war.[26] Roberts, the chairman of the special committee, then sought again

[25] *Annals of Congress,* Thirteenth Congress, First Session, 465.

[26] This is shown by Roberts' amendment (*House Journal,* Thirteenth Congress, First Session, 113).

to remove this restriction and insert in place
of it, "if they shall have resided therein [in
the United States] for the continued term of
five years immediately preceding their admission as citizens in manner aforesaid." Kennedy had suggested this measure to those who
opposed the admission of any whose declaration had not been made before June 18, 1812,
as a compromise that would be acceptable.
His side were now driven to urge it as a last
resort in defense of their contention. The
Roberts amendment failed, as did also an
effort to admit of later declaration by those
who "had intermarried with a citizen of the
United States." The bill became a law on
July 30, 1813.[27] It was entitled: "An act supplementary to the acts heretofore passed on
the subject of an uniform rule of naturalization." It provided "that persons resident
within the United States, or the Territories
thereof," at the outbreak of the war, "who had
before that day made a declaration according
to law" of intent to become citizens of the
United States, or who, by the existing laws,
were entitled to become citizens without
making a declaration, might be admitted to
become citizens thereof, notwithstanding they
should be alien enemies, at the time and in the

[27] *House Journal*, Thirteenth Congress, First Session, 113, 114,
130, 131, 135, 141. A Senate amendment was disagreed to.

manner prescribed by the laws heretofore passed on that subject; provided that the act was not to be construed to interfere with the removal, etc., of any alien enemy before his actual naturalization.[28]

In summing up the foregoing history, we note that the first bill simply removed the enemy disability from those in the United States at the beginning of the war (June 18, 1812); but it was amended to limit declarations to six months after its passage. This bill received a pocket veto. The second bill removed the alien-enemy disability from all who were in the United States on June 1, 1812, but required a declaration of intention within nine months. It was amended by the senate too late in the session for further action in the House. The third bill originated in the Senate. It removed the alien-enemy disability from those who were in the United States on June 18, 1812, but any required declaration of intention was to be made within nine months. The House, after a lively struggle within itself, succeeded in limiting the application of the measure to those whose declaration of intention was made before the outbreak of the war, or who needed to make no declaration.

[28] *Statutes at Large*, III, 53.

CHAPTER VIII

AN ACT CONCERNING EVIDENCE

During the discussion of the bill for the naturalization of alien enemies, Dana (Conn.) made repeated attempts in the Senate to secure consideration of a bill concerning evidence in cases of naturalization. He introduced it on July 19, 1813, and, failing to gain a hearing for it so late in the session, secured its postponement to the first week in December.[1] In the following session, however, he introduced a new bill.[2] Three weeks later he secured its reference to a committee of which he was chairman, and reported it unchanged, but could get for it no other consideration than a second postponement over the recess.[3] Early in the first session of the new Congress in 1815 he renewed his efforts, with better success. After amendment in both House and Senate, his bill became a law March 22, 1816.[4] The title was: "An act relative to evidence in cases of naturalization."

[1] *Annals of Congress,* Thirteenth Congress, First Session, 59, 62, 79; July 19, 21, 30, 1813.

[2] December 23.

[3] *Annals of Congress,* Thirteenth Congress, Second Session, 563, 571, 759, 775; December 23, 1813; January 10, April 18, 1814.

[4] *Senate Journal,* Fourteenth Congress, First Session, 50, 55, 68, 73, 77, 83; *House Journal,* Fourteenth Congress, First Session, 164, 305, 312, 336, 411, 418, 496.

It provided that the certificate of report and registry required by the act of 1802, and also a certificate of the declaration of intention, should be exhibited by every alien who should have arrived in the United States after June 18, 1812, and that each should be recited at full length in the record of the court admitting such alien to citizenship. Otherwise he should not be deemed to have complied with the conditions required for becoming a citizen of the United States. Any pretended admission of such citizen, after the promulgation of the act, without such recital of each certificate at full length, should be of no validity. Any person admitted without a certificate must prove to the satisfaction of the court that he was a resident in the United States before April 14, 1802, and had resided therein continuously since. The proof of his residence for the five years immediately preceding his admission must be by the oath or affirmation of citizens of the United States, who must be named in the record as witnesses. The fact of continuous residence must be stated in the record, also all places of residence for five years. A record of naturalization without these particulars should not entitle a person to be considered a citizen.[5]

5 *Statutes at Large*, III, 258.

In January, 1816, Wilson (N. J.) submitted
for the consideration of the Senate a resolution for a committee to inquire into the expediency of revising and digesting the several
acts of Congress on the subject of naturalization, or of compiling and publishing the said
acts, and distributing the same to the officers
of courts authorized to issue certificates of
naturalization. The outcome of this was a
resolution [6] that the secretary of state have
printed four thousand copies of the laws then
in force on the subject of naturalization, and
send two copies of each to the clerk of each
federal or state court authorized to naturalize,
to each collector of customs, and to each marshal of a United States judicial district. Remaining copies should go to the executive department and the Library of Congress.[7]

During a debate in the House in committee
of the whole, in 1816, on a bill to incorporate
subscribers to the national bank, Randolph
(Va.) moved to add the word "native" in the
clause that limited the choice of directors to
citizens of the United States, thus making it
read "native citizens." This motion was
agreed to (ayes, 68) without debate. When

---

[6] Approved April 16, 1816.

[7] *Senate Journal,* Fourteenth Congress, First Session, 77, 79,
371, 422, 478; *House Journal,* Fourteenth Congress, First Session,
636; *Annals of Congress,* Fourteenth Congress, First Session, 1918.

the clause providing for the appointment of
directors for branch banks was reached, a
similar motion was made to insert "native"
in a similar provision. Calhoun then objected
to the amendment. He said that it was the
first attempt that had been made to discriminate between native and naturalized citizens.
The constitution recognized no such distinction, except in eligibility to the highest office,
and he could see no reason for introducing at
that time so odious and unprecedented a distinction. Randolph replied to Calhoun at
considerable length, and, in the words of *Niles
Register,* "he inveighed with much acrimony
against the whole class of naturalized citizens." He declared that the United States
owed to its naturalization laws the spirit of
faction by which it had been torn for twenty
years, and along with it the war just over.
Protecting foreign seamen had also grown out
of it. How long the country must endure this
foreign yoke in its most odious and disgusting
form he could not tell! He would much rather
be ruled by the British Parliament than by
British subjects in America. They must teach
the people of Europe that all they must hope
to receive in America was protection. They
must have no share in the government.
Wright replied warmly to Randolph, and this

motion was lost without division.   When the
bill came before the House, Calhoun secured
the rejection of the first amendment also, by
a vote of 44 to 67, although Randolph again
advocated it in a short speech.[8]

[8] *Annals of Congress,* Fourteenth Congress, First Session, 1152,
1153, 1200; *Niles Register,* X, 31, 47; March 6 and 11, 1816.

CHAPTER IX

EXPATRIATION

In giving a summary of the laws of Virginia in 1781, Jefferson wrote[1] that "citizens may divest themselves of that character by declaring, by solemn deed, or in open court, that they mean to expatriate themselves, and no longer to be citizens of this state." He added to this summary of the laws the statement that the first assembly after Virginia became a state appointed three men to revise the code. Among the most remarkable alterations they proposed was "to define with precision the rules whereby aliens should become citizens, and citizens make themselves aliens."[2]

In the summer of 1817,[3] a few months before the exhaustive debate on the subject of expatriation occurred in Congress, Jefferson wrote from Monticello to Dr. John Manners:

My opinion on the right of expatriation has been so long ago as the year 1776, consigned to record in the act of the Virginia code, drawn by myself, recognizing the right expressly, and prescribing the mode of exercising it. The evidence of this natural right like that of the right to life, liberty, and the use of our faculties, the pursuit of happiness, is not left to the feeble and sophistical investigations

[1] Jefferson, *Writings,* III, 240; in his *Notes on Virginia.*
[2] *Ibid.,* 242, 243.   [3] June 12.

of the reason, but is impressed on the sense of every man. We do not claim these under the charters of Kings or legislators, but under the King of Kings. If he has made it a law in the nature of man to pursue his own happiness, he has left him free in the choice of place as well as mode; and we may safely call upon the whole body of English jurists to produce the map on which Nature has traced, for each individual, the geographical line which she forbids him to cross in pursuit of happiness. It certainly does not exist in his mind. Where, then, is it? I believe, too, I might safely affirm, that there is not another nation, civilized or savage, which has ever denied this natural right. I doubt if there is another which refuses it exercise.[4]

Jefferson had, while president, occasion to make practical application of his views upon this subject in a case in which he maintained the binding force of the doctrine against a man who wished to free himself from the consequences of his own act in having formerly availed himself of it. Jefferson wrote to his secretary of the treasury (Gallatin) :[5]

The Attorney-General being absent, we must decide for ourselves the question raised by Colonel Newton's letter, whether Mr. Cooper can own a registered vessel? or, in other words, whether he is a citizen of the United States.

I hold the right of expatriation to be inherent in every man by the laws of nature. and incapable of being rightfully taken from him even by the united will of every other person in the nation. If the laws have provided no particular mode by which the right of expatriation may be exercised, the individual may do it by any effectual and

4 Jefferson, *Writings,* X, 87.   5 June 26, 1806.

unequivocal act or declaration. The laws of Virginia have provided a mode; Mr. Cooper is said to have exercised his right solemnly and exactly according to that mode, and to have departed from the Commonwealth; whereupon the law declares that "he shall thenceforth be deemed no citizen." Returning afterwards he returns an alien, and must proceed to make himself a citizen if he desires it, as every other alien does. At present he can hold no lands, receive nor transmit any inheritance, nor enjoy any other right peculiar to a citizen.

The general government has nothing to do with this question. Congress may by the Constitution " establish an uniform rule of naturalization," that is, by what rule an alien may become a citizen. But they cannot take from a citizen his natural right of divesting himself of the character of a citizen by expatriation.[6]

From many points of view this is a most interesting letter. It unhesitatingly accepted the view that a state was competent to legislate in the matter of expatriation, involving, as Jefferson held that it must, the loss of federal citizenship. The Virginia law being in force and applying to this person, the appeal to it was, from Jefferson's point of view, absolutely necessary, and apparently none the less acceptable. Perhaps he did not decide the question as to whether Congress could also indicate a valid mode of expatriation. At any rate, his language seems to necessitate the view that it could not establish an exclusive mode, although he took the position that the

[6] Jefferson, *Writings,* VIII, 454.

legal mode or modes, when there were such, were exclusive of all others. "The general government has nothing to do with this question," is indefinite as to whether it applies to the particular case Jefferson had in hand, or to the general question of expatriation. His last sentence might seem to have been framed to avoid expressing a decision upon this point. The citizen character lost by expatriation was totally lost, and the person became an alien. That character was not resumable at will, nor by consent of the government, but only through the full process of naturalization. He had no question, such as Madison once expressed,[7] as to the right of an expatriated American to become naturalized under the laws that applied to foreigners.

In the summer of 1797 considerable discussion on the subject of expatriation occurred in the House committee of the whole during the consideration of a bill to prevent citizens of the United States from entering foreign service. We are informed merely that Rutledge (S. C.), W. Smith (S. C.), Dayton (N. J.), Brooks (N. Y.), Otis (Mass.), and Kittera (Pa.) spoke in favor of marking out a way for expatriation. On the other hand,

[7] See p. 54. An opinion of Hamilton on the subject of expatriation has been quoted, in another connection, on page 3.

Coit (Conn.) was probably successful in his motion to strike out a section declaring that for the due execution of a portion of the act it was expedient to define and ascertain the mode in which a citizen might dissolve the ties of citizenship.[8]

Great interest and much feeling on the subject of expatriation were aroused by the decision [9] in the case of Isaac Williams, who was tried [10] in the Circuit Court of the District of Connecticut for accepting a French naval commission, contrary to the law laid down in Art. XXI of the Jay Treaty, that subjects or citizens of the one country should not accept commissions from a foreign state at war with the other. Williams claimed that he was appointed to a place in the French navy in 1792, and was naturalized in France the same autumn. He had only visited in the United States, less than six months, in 1796. The court held that "the common law of this country remains the same as it was before the revolution," that all the members of a civil community were bound to each other by a compact, and that one of the parties to the compact could not dissolve it by his own act.

[8] *Annals of Congress,* Fifth Congress, First Session, 348; June 20 and 21, 1797.

[9] Rendered by Chief Justice Ellsworth, of the United States Supreme Court.

[10] 1799.

There had been no consent or default on the part of the community. Nor did he admit the implied consent that had been argued from its policy, condition, and acts. Their country had no inhabitants to spare. They naturalized, but did not inquire as to the relation still sustained to the other country. "But this implies no consent of the government that our own citizens should expatriate themselves." The fault and folly of embarrassing himself are his own.[11]

Various articles upon the subject appeared. One in the *South Carolina Gazette*,[12] signed "South Carolina Planter," was written by Charles Pinckney, and was called forth by another case, that of Mackay and Nicks vs. the Polacre Ship "Adams," condemned by the British. The claimant was held to be a British subject because he was not admitted a citizen of the United States until March, 1796,[13] and hence could not be considered, with respect to England, a citizen of the United States, to permit of his trading with the British enemy. On the right to change nationality Pinckney quoted Cicero as saying that "the way is open from every state to ours and from ours to

[11] Wharton's *State Trials*, 652; quoted in part in Snow's *Cases on International Law*, 215.

[12] October 10, 1799.

[13] He had settled in the United States in 1792; the war began in February, 1793.

every state." He cited Grotius, and quoted Vattel as saying that a man may leave his country "except when he cannot abandon it without doing it a remarkable prejudice." In case of naval war or distant expeditions no danger was threatened at home, and England had been at war more than half of the last century. The law of England and of Russia infringed upon the right of naturalization. The United States must protect the commerce of its new subjects, or their grant of citizenship was a public deception.

The Williams decision was printed in the *South Carolina Gazette* for November 28, 1799. A week later a reply, entitled "On Expatriation," signed "A Federalist," appeared in the same paper. This writer urged that the common law, on which the decision was based, had been greatly modified by the Revolution. He admitted that the government was based on a compact, and that one could not dissolve it. But the only compact with American citizens was the Constitution. It contained no express principle against a citizen of the United States joining another state. Posterity were not bound in their personal liberty by the Constitution when they left the country. An article in the same paper a year later [14] blamed

[14] October 16, 1800.

the Federalists for supporting the Williams
decision.

A series of articles in the *Aurora*, [15] signed
"T. C. of Northumberland," discussed the subject of expatriation. New light had come to
English law on this subject from the revolutionary period. In earlier European history
the people gradually came to be considered
the subjects or property of their rulers, and
from this fact allegiance was considered to be
perpetual. Yet writers on general law had
always claimed exceptions. These had gradually been extended. This progress of opinion
caused a presumption that the right of expatriation was to be more universally acknowledged. The latest writers were fifty
years old and from despotic countries. As
general arguments in favor of expatriation he
noted exceptions allowed by the writers, as
follows: (1) the case of a government plainly
tyrannical; (2) religious duties, etc., being
prohibited; (3) extreme economic reasons,
such as the usual means of subsistence failing;
(4) failure of duty by the state (also to the
state); (5) the fundamental laws being violated. He suggested also to be added to these:
(1) desire of bettering fortune; (2) demands
of health, relations, etc. Thus he found that

[15] January 22, 24, 25, 1800.

exceptions applied to nearly every case and destroyed the law. Moreover, the extreme of the law would show that no allegiance was due to any of the existing governments. Only the first government could be lawful. Again, the law directly opposed every revolution. It was unnecessary to any good government. And again, the being able and willing was implied in the making of all valid contracts. These illustrations indicate the trend of the thought of the time.

The failure of Burwell's attempt in 1808 to enact "that all citizens shall be considered such no longer than while they actually reside within the United States, and also that if any citizen shall expatriate himself, he shall *ipso facto,* be deemed an alien, and, ever after, be incapable of becoming a citizen," has been mentioned.[16]

An expatriation bill before Congress in 1817 led to an exhaustive debate upon the subject. The bill "by which the right of citizenship may be relinquished"[17] was reported[18] by a committee[19] appointed[20] to inquire into the ex-

[16] See p. 116.

[17] Probably the language of its title.

[18] December 22, 1817.

[19] Robertson (La.), Mason (Mass.), Poindexter (Miss.), Ross (Pa.), and Floyd (Va.).

[20] December 15, 1817.

pediency of providing by law for the exercise of the right of expatriation.[21]

In making the motion for the committee, Robertson said that he had offered a similar resolution some years before, during the war. The war question had made a decision necessary. England had treated many prisoners as traitors, and the United States could not consistently retaliate, for she had not recognized in her own citizens the right that she demanded that Great Britain should concede to hers. In the Williams case a man had been fined and imprisoned by the United States courts, on the ground that he could not divest himself of United States citizenship. It was proper for the legislature to decide so important a question. Under a treaty with Spain,[22] a citizen of the United States holding a commission from any government at war with Spain while we are at peace with her, is considered as a pirate. They were not neutral as between Spain and her colonies so long as a citizen of the United States in fighting for the colonies was a pirate, and in fighting against them was not. He wished to see American citizens at perfect liberty to become citizens elsewhere on

[21] *House Journal,* Fifteenth Congress, First Session, 50, 73.

[22] Art. XIV of the treaty of 1795 is referred to. No citizen of either nation is to take commission or letter of marque from the enemy of the other.

any terms the other nation might prescribe.
He favored the principle involved, and the
existing circumstances required it. His resolution was adopted without opposition.[23]

The bill reported contained two sections.
The first section provided

That whensoever any citizen of the United States shall, by
a declaration in writing, made and executed in the district
court of the United States, within the state where he
resides, in open court to be by said court entered of record,
declare that he relinquishes the character of a citizen, and
shall depart out of the United States, such person shall,
from the time of his departure, be considered as having
exercised his right of expatriation, and shall thenceforth
be considered no citizen.[24]

The second section enacted

that such person shall be held as an alien forever after, and
shall not resume the rights of citizenship without going
through the same process of naturalization as other citizens.[25]

When the bill first came up in committee
of the whole,[26] Lowndes (S. C.) remarked that
it dealt with "a subject of too much importance to be acted on by so thin a house," and
it was postponed. Robertson (Ky) opened
the long debate.[27] The same proposition years
ago had met with opposition both expected

[23] *Annals of Congress,* Fifteenth Congress, First Session, 448.

[24] *House Journal,* Fifteenth Congress, First Session, 284.

[25] *Annals of Congress,* Fifteenth Congress, First Session, 495.
The quotation is taken from a summary of the bill.

[26] December 24, 1817.   [27] December 26, 1817.

and unexpected. It had been considered, as most principles not borrowed from the common law (to which he alluded in a very sarcastic way), as fraught with great mischief. It interfered with negotiations, and encouraged desertion, piracy, and every sin in the Decalogue. But he was now redeeming his pledge to bring it up again. It was not borrowed from England, and it might prove beneficial to the patriots of South America, and odious to the friends of Ferdinand. It might rescue citizens from the crime of piracy attributed to them by treaty. Yet he should press the principle.

He considered expatriation to be an acknowledged natural right, and demanded that opponents show proof of indelible allegiance. Man had natural rights, governments had none. The friends of liberty were not innovators. The right of the government to perpetual allegiance did not exist here—where was it in the Constitution? His principle, liberty, was in the Constitution. It was inalienable, and was a necessary consequence of naturalization. He denounced the absurdity of their right to naturalize and the right of another government to the allegiance of the person naturalized. He had seen some ingenious quibbling in favor of that nonsense.

Perhaps the right of expatriation had never been denied in ancient or modern days except by English, Chinese, and, it might be, Hottentot governments. Thor and Woden were believed to be the authors of the principle of indelible allegiance—the idea had originated in the dark ages. Expatriation had been practiced by Jews, Greeks (Lycurgus), and Romans. He quoted as Cicero's this language:

O glorious right by the Divine favor obtained for us by our ancestors in the commencement of the Roman name; by which no man can be the citizen of more than one country; by which no man can be compelled to leave it against his will, nor remain in it against his inclination! This is the firmest foundation of our liberty, that every man should have an absolute power to retain or abandon his right at his election.

France in 1793 had made the loss of citizenship follow from naturalization in a foreign country or the acceptance of office from other than a popular government. Since the right of expatriation had been denied in America,[28] and the enjoyment of it denied when the right was admitted,[29] it was necessary for Congress to secure them by law. The law proposed was in substance a copy of the Virginia act. It did not presume to give the right, but pointed out the manner of exercising it.

Anderson (Ky.) had no doubt of the exist-

[28] Case of I. Williams.   [29] 3 Dallas, 133.

ence of the right; probably it would not be denied or doubted. But he would examine the question of constitutional power of prescribing rules for its exercise before that of the policy of so doing. Such power did not exist. It could not be fairly inferred, nor was it necessary or convenient for the exercise of other powers. The grant of the power to naturalize did not imply its correlative, any more than the power to borrow money implied that to lend money, or import duty power implied export duty power.

They must also distinguish between acknowledging a right and granting power to prescribe the manner of enjoying the right. The proposed Thirteenth Amendment, excluding any citizen from office under a foreign power, with the penalty that he "shall cease to be a citizen of the United States," had been sanctioned by twelve states. That Congress deemed there was a necessity for that amendment was a recognition of the fact that they could not declare the acts that should be equivalent to renunciation of citizenship. Yet that was what the bill in effect did. Rights that the Constitution created might be controlled in their exercise by law, but this right was not created by it. If this power existed in any legislative body, it was in the state legislatures. Some of them had already exercised it; denying it to them would lead to a conflict with Virginia.

This power of declaring what should disfranchise a citizen of a state was too great a one to concede to the general government. It was a question whether the unrestrained enjoyment of the right was not better and more fully secured by denying to anybody the power to legislate regarding it. Legislation to secure rights was often unnecessary, and often dangerous. Their perfect enjoyment depended upon the entire absence of legislative control. Power could be claimed that would enable Congress to require a mode of expatriation so inconvenient as to amount to an entire denial of the right. Foreign legislators might even require forms and notice of intention. They were then recognizing the validity of British statutes that held the emigrant to be bound by his foreign allegiance. No countenance should be given to the idea that their naturalized citizens had not every privilege and safety. Emigration was rapid among the states and mere departure forfeited the character of citizenship. No state had deemed a law to be necessary to define the act of forfeiture.

They must rest simply upon the character

of the government to keep their citizens. He would never raise legal fences against immigration, nor have any artificial barriers to keep men in; yet he thought the bill before them was both unnecessary and unconstitutional.

Johnson (Ky.) declared that the Declaration of Independence recognized the right of expatriation. Denial of it was not modern, but originated in the days of feudal tenures and oath of fealty, perpetual fealty leading to perpetual allegiance. Not a nation in Europe refused to let its citizens or subjects become citizens and subjects of another nation. The right was as sacred and inalienable as any right. But what became of the power to naturalize when the right of expatriation was denied? Judicial decisions against the right made legislation to point out the mode of its exercise indispensable.

Pindall (Va.) had understood the friends of the bill as viewing it only as providing a record of a legal expatriation, but their complaints against the courts, etc., proved that this was not so. Was it intended to expatriate from the general government only and not from the states? Or from either one? Or both? Congress, he declared, had no control over state allegiance, and state allegiance secured to a person general privileges. There were no considerations of policy or of expediency to recommend the bill. It would be a shelter for the traitor and the pirate, and its passage would involve the commission of fraud against their treaties, several of which contained the article that was in the Spanish treaty. No one would ever avail himself of the provisions of the bill without motives of idleness or criminality. He had never heard of any country that granted naturalization only after an expatriation according to law. If it were otherwise, citizens might have an excuse for the use of that bill. He was willing to grant the right of expatriation, but not that of fighting against one's country. Something was still owed to the former citizenship. There was no hint in the Constitution of an oath of abjuration. As to the difficulties growing out of double allegiance, they might well leave the individual to the result of his own entangling, and explain anomalies by reference to the abnormal state of war and the force it necessitated. The awkwardness of the conception was due to forsaking the old view of expatriation as involving a prejudice (disgrace) rather than a right. Virginia, the only state adopting expatriation as a policy, did so at the close of the Revolutionary war, and the fact was an evidence of her magnanimity.

Little harm had resulted from her action, and
yet her statute was better regarded as a mu-
seum ornament than as a legislative precedent.
The bill before them would do much evil.

Lowndes (S. C.) moved to strike out sec.
1 of the bill.[30] It would bring no benefits and
was unconstitutional. The existence of the
right was admitted, and was sufficiently recognized by Congress. So delicate a power as
that of regulating it should be expressly granted. It would release from all liabilities and
also release from all privileges. The view
that the Constitution should control the rights
of citizens was upheld by the proposed amendment already referred to. As there was no
law to regulate the exercise of rebellion, so
no legislation was necessary to secure the
right of expatriation, even if the Constitution
had given the needed power. What did the
treaty provision mean more than the loss of
protection? Robertson (La.) replied at
length to Lowndes. Henry Clay took the
same view as Robertson as to the Spanish
treaty and referred to a piracy trial at Boston
as illustrating its effect.

An all-day discussion [31] ensued on the motion to strike out the first section. McLane

[30] This motion was, of course, intended to kill the bill.
[31] February 28, 1818.

(Del.) declared it to be unnecessary to affirm or deny the right to expatriate. He would seek to show that the measure was unconstitutional and would be inefficient. Assuming the right, it was a civil one whose exercise must be consistent with mutual obligations. He dwelt on the states'-rights argument against the constitutionality of the measure. Even if released by the general government, a person continued to be a citizen of his state. An indefinite supremacy over the personal rights and effects of individuals was implied in the measure. It was inexpedient for many reasons, novel and unreasonable. It concerned a delicate and extreme right shaking the foundations of civil government. The exercise of the right presupposed a fault in the country, and was always to be deplored. They should not make that exercise easy, weakening the love of country. A better policy was to encourage immigration. The right claimed exonerated man from every sort of civil obligation, and legalized treason, plunder, and spoil. Their duties to their own dignity and to the world forbade that. The effects of the law in the case of a crisis at home might be serious. Many would evade the danger by means of it.

Johnson replied that McLane's arguments

rested on an old feudal doctrine unknown in England till the time of William I. No Virginian would abandon his country in danger. Citizens of the United States did possess the right in question in most ample, unlimited, and unlimitable degree. They had derived it from heaven. The decision in the Williams case was an act of tyranny and oppression, for which the judge ought to have been impeached. England's conduct in making two years' service in the navy constitute a person a citizen asserted the right. To presume to naturalize, and at the same time to deny the right of expatriation, ought to subject a government to ridicule and scorn. Nevertheless, he believed that the bill was unconstitutional.

Cobb (Ga.) said that the object of the bill was not to change any known law, but rather to declare that the principle of perpetual allegiance had no force in the United States. The constitutional right to point out the manner of exercising it was clearly incidental to the power of establishing a uniform rule of naturalization, and necessarily resulted from it. The powers were correlative, and the one could not be conceived without the other. In the case of naturalization, the law only prescribed the rule for the act of the individual.

It was also so in expatriation, for the bill imposed no restriction on the right. They need not be anxious about the fate of the citizen who became an outlaw by his own act. He could not conceive of any effect of the measure on state sovereignty. After renouncing the citizenship of all the states, one could not . claim to be a citizen of any one of them. Prince Eugene, Marshal Saxe, and General Patkul had all fought against the country of their birth. Had no difficulties arisen, there had been no necessity for legislating upon this subject.

A decision to strike out sec. 1 was reached by a small majority of the committee of the whole. The House concurred in this action. A sharp contest then ensued to save the bill, Johnson and Robertson claiming that it was yet capable of amendment. Others opposed this effort as utterly unparliamentary, and adjournment was finally accomplished with a motion by Johnson pending, to lay the bill on the table. Later [32] Johnson withdrew his motion, and proposed as a substitute for the remaining section of the bill a new measure, as follows:

That whereas sundry persons who had been citizens of the United States of America, and who had exercised the

[32] March 2, 1818.

right of dissolving the connection which bound them to the United States in the character of citizens, by voluntarily and regularly becoming citizens or subjects of other governments, have been held bound to answer in the character of citizens, in the courts of the United States, for offences alleged to have been committed subsequently to the exercise of this right; and for which citizens only would be amenable, in the said courts. And whereas, in the Declaration of Independence, of the thirteen United States of America, the following truths are held to be self-evident, that all men are created equal, that they are endowed by their Creator with certain unalienable rights; that among these are life, liberty, and the pursuit of happiness. Therefore be it enacted and it is hereby expressly enacted and declared that all men do possess the right to seek their happiness in any climate, and under any form of government they may elect; and that, consequently, the right to dissolve the connexion which binds the individual to the government of the United States, in the character of citizen, and to form a similar connexion with any other government, is equally unalienable, and founded on truth equally self-evident.

Williams (N. C.) declared it to be beyond the constitutional power of the House to pass the measure, and that every honest man in the country would disdain to take advantage of it. Should they then legislate for the vicious? No man in the House was a stronger advocate of the right of expatriation than he was, but they could not regulate it without circumscribing it. It was a right reserved to the people. They were proposing to legislate fellow-citizens into aliens. He touched a very fundamental question when he said that his opponents held that the right of expatriation attached to the individual upon his leaving his native country, while those with him held that it attached upon his becoming the citizen or subject of another country. The difference was as to a point of time. All persons must be subject to the laws of some society. The United States could not make a person a subject of Great Britain, nor Great Britain make one a subject of the United States. If an American became a subject of Britain, it was by British law; and this right to become a British subject the United States acknowledged.

Abbott (Ga.) favored the amendment as a mere declaratory expression of Congress. It might have some weight with the courts. Johnson also declared that the question before them then was a mere declaratory provision, the object being to exclude a wrong inference from the last vote. It prescribed no rule and no act. No construction of it as legislating a person out of his rights was possible. After other unreported speeches, a motion to postpone indefinitely both bill and amendment failed: yeas, 73; nays, 88.[33] A motion to substitute the word "declared" for "enacted" in the enacting clause was lost.[34]

[33] *House Journal*, Fifteenth Congress, First Session, 289.

[34] *Annals of Congress*, Fifteenth Congress, First Session, 1093. Vote, 67 to 76.

Again an amendment was offered in an effort to save a part of the contention of the supporters of the bill, and provide a measure that
a majority of the House would accept. Robertson moved to strike out the second section
and insert the following:

> That in all prosecutions which may hereafter be insti-
> tuted against any person for having engaged in military, or
> naval service, for or against any foreign power, when with-
> out the jurisdiction of the United States, who, before the
> commission of the fact with which he may stand charged,
> shall have been a citizen of the United States, but shall
> have exercised his right of expatriation, by becoming the
> citizen or subject of any foreign state or community by
> adoption, it shall be lawful for such person to give such
> fact of expatriation in evidence, upon the general issue,
> and if upon the trial of such person so charged as aforesaid,
> he shall prove such fact to the satisfaction of the jury, he
> shall be discharged from such prosecution.[35]

As a result of this amendment, action on the
bill was deferred to give time for its consideration. When the bill was next before the
House,[36] Forsythe moved to insert between
"by" and "becoming" in the phrase "by becoming the citizen or subject of any foreign
state," the words "recording in the office of
the clerk of some one of the district courts of
the United States, a declaration that such is
his intention twelve months prior to."

[35] *House Journal*, Fifteenth Congress, First Session, 291.
[36] March 4, 1817.

Robertson's amendment had proposed the test of foreign citizenship to determine expatriation. He had thus occupied the ground of Williams (N. C.), only that he sought to add to it the sanction of a law with a limited application. Forsythe's amendment involved a long step back toward the measure first proposed, and was certain to revive a string of constitutional objections. It was lost, apparently without division. A motion followed to strike out "for or," and thus limit the application of the measure to the case of service "against any foreign power." Thus a right to fight against one's native country would have been refused recognition, and emphasis given to fighting against a foreign power. The motion was supported by Terry and Coulson, and opposed by Edwards, Robertson, and Lowndes. It failed to pass by a large majority. "For or against any foreign power" remained, but a motion in the same direction as the last one, avoiding some of the inferences that it would have involved, passed. The phrase "and not in hostility against the said states" was inserted after the words "United States," by a vote of 65 to 59.

Several other amendments were then agreed to, the result of which was to eliminate all direct reference to expatriation. The clause "shall have exercised his right of expatriation, by becoming the citizen or subject of any foreign state or community by adoption," was changed to read "shall have bona fide and voluntarily become the citizen or subject of any foreign state, while within its jurisdiction." This result was reached step by step. "Or community" and "by adoption" were dropped out separately, and "bona fide and voluntarily," and "while within its jurisdiction," were separately added. In the original amendment, "give such fact of expatriation" was changed to "give the fact that he has been naturalized in some foreign state."

After being thus amended, the amendment was substituted for sec. 2 (all that remained of the original bill), by a vote of 93 to 61.[37]

Sec. 2, which thus disappeared, had made the renaturalization of persons expatriated the condition of their restoration to citizenship. Williams (N. C.) offered at this point a new section declaring tl at no person who availed himself of the privileges of the bill and became expatriated should ever after be permitted to be naturalized as a citizen of the United States. His motion was rejected.

Robertson opposed the bill as it had been amended, mainly the clause that denied a

[37] *House Journal*, Fifteenth Congress, First Session, 298; *Annals of Congress*, Fifteenth Congress, First Session, 1104-6.

right to fight for the country of adoption against the native country. His opposition led to the reconsideration and defeat of the amendment by which the phrase "and not in hostility against the said states" had been inserted. The final action taken at the end of this long course of debate and maneuvering was to reject the bill by a vote of 64 to 75.[38] No other serious attempt to define the right of expatriation occurred for fifty years.

Niles Register[39] quoted the *National Intelligencer* in reference to what the latter called "the animated debate" on the expatriation bill. It said that the sense of the House appeared to be

against legislating on the question of expatriation, on the ground, that to prescribe the mode of exercising a fundamental right is to assume the power of limiting it, which power, it is contended, does not belong to Congress.

The question was one surrounded with difficulties, but the able debate would have shed a light that might lead to a

definitive rule on a point regarding which it appears, that the decision of Congress and the opinion of the courts of the United States are at variance.

A few later references to the subject may be mentioned in closing this chapter. Editorial

[38] *House Journal*, Fifteenth Congress, First Session, 300; *Annals of Congress,* Fifteenth Congress, First Session, 1107.

[39] XIV, 27; February 27, 1818.

articles appeared at different times in *Niles Register* on the subject of expatriation. In one the editor wrote: "Without expatriation there cannot be naturalization." [40] In another the "perpetual allegiance doctrine" of "praters of royalty" was attacked, and proofs were offered that even Russia was naturalizing.[41] A similar and more forcible article was based upon the report in London papers of the naturalization of George Leopold Coburg by Parliament "in the space of six minutes." Perpetual allegiance was asserted to be "the most abominable doctrine that ever was held forth." For anti-slavery people to hold it "was too impudent to be borne with patience."[42] An article entitled "Who Are Citizens?" held that Americans who had served Mexico in war were expatriated and should not vote in the United States. Either they were not citizens or they were pirates; and yet a law was needed to provide regularly for expatriation.[43]

John Quincy Adams wrote in his diary in 1824 that Calhoun doubted the right of expatriation, declared that he had always been against it in feeling, and had never committed himself upon it during the War of 1812.

[40] *Niles Register*, V, 237; 1813.
[41] *Ibid.*, X, 167; 1816.   [42] *Ibid.*, X, 170; 1816.
[43] *Ibid.*, XXXV, 162; November 8, 1828.

Adams agreed with him in sentiment, but thought that they had foreclosed that argument against themselves by the oath renouncing foreign allegiance, which they required from foreigners as the condition of naturalization. A few days later the subject came up again between them, and Calhoun was emphatically of the opinion that native-born citizens of the United States had no such right, except Virginians. They had it by virtue of a law of their state.[44]

The limitation of this opinion to native-born citizens involves a peculiar distinction. The inference from it is that the United States, by requiring renunciation of former allegiance from foreigners, had conferred upon them a right (not shared by native-born citizens) to claim the principle of expatriation against the government, if they should wish to do so. Probably the suggestion given by Adams helped Calhoun to reach this conclusion. The suggestion as to Virginians is a striking illustration of the controlling character of the states'-rights idea in the mind of Calhoun at that early period. The complete denial of any real federal citizenship, or at least of any such citizenship without the domain of ordinary state control, is fundamental to it.

[44] J. Q. Adams, *Memoirs*, VI, 381, 385; June 10 and 13, 1824.

The United States Senate in 1839 [45] referred
and ordered printed a resolution of the Michigan General Assembly urging the adoption
of measures to insure that foreign powers
recognize the rights of naturalized citizens.
In substance, it was as follows: Whereas the
constitution of Michigan is pre-eminently characterized by its spirit of liberality to the foreign emigrant,[46] and it is just, right, and proper
that no envious distinctions should exist in
the United States between adopted and native
citizens, and the free right of expatriation is
yet unrecognized in treaties with foreign
nations, subjecting, in case of war, many adopted
citizens to the peril of being deemed and treated
as traitors; Resolved: That our senators are instructed and our representative is requested
to use their efforts for the adoption of such
measures as will insure the recognition, by
foreign powers, of the absolute citizenship of
all foreigners naturalized by the existing laws
of the United States. This resolution, by its
reference to treaties with foreign powers on
the subject of expatriation, forecasted clearly
the ultimate solution of the question.

[45] (341) *Senate Documents,* Twenty-fifth Congress, Third Session, No. 262 (February 25, 1839); (337) *Senate Journal,* Twenty-
fifth Congress, Third Session, 270; and (353) ibid., Twenty-sixth
Congress, First Session, 84.

[46] Every "white male inhabitant" of legal age who was "a
resident of the State" at the time of the adoption of the first
Michigan constitution in 1835 was given the suffrage (Poore,
Charters and *Constitutions,* I, 984).

An accompanying memorial [47] of naturalized citizens of Michigan prayed for measures
to secure the recognition of their rights as
citizens of the United States. They had sev-
ered former relations, transferred their allegiance, and were attached by strongest ties
and by solemn oath to the United States government. By requiring them to bear arms
it virtually guaranteed to them the full and
equal rights of natives. Yet British jurists
and courts insisted on the doctrine of perpetual allegiance, which was at war with their
equal rights. The enlightenment and liberal
policy of the British cabinet at that time [48]
justified belief in their favorable consideration
of the measures desired. A few weeks before
the resolution of the Michigan Legislature
was received, the Senate had referred the petition of a naturalized Irishman, who had escaped from Canada after being sentenced for
treason for aiding in the Canadian rebellion.
He asked that the rights of naturalized citizens of the United States might be ascertained
and defined. England's laws were character-
izing one-fourth of the population of the United
States as her perpetual subjects. The United

[47] (341) *Senate Documents,* Twenty-fifth Congress, Third Session, No. 263.

[48] This was the second Melbourne ministry. Palmerston, John
Russell, and T. B. Macaulay were in the leading offices.

States should settle forever their status in time of peace, for in case of war with England they could enlist only subject to treason penalties.[49]

A petition of Sherlock S. Gregory, Rensselaer County, New York, was presented in the House in 1837 by John Quincy Adams. The author prayed to be considered an alien, or stranger in the land, so long as slavery existed and the wrongs of the Indians were unrequited or unrepented of.[50]

In January, 1858, a resolution was agreed to in the House directing the Committee on Judiciary to inquire if any, and what, legislation by Congress might be proper to define what acts should, or should not, work expatriation or severance of allegiance by citizens of the United States;

and also whether provision by law ought to be made for reinvesting with citizenship such persons, born in the United States, as may have assumed allegiance or citizenship to any foreign government.[1]

Two years later[52] a similar resolution received the same reference, and with it the further query whether provision by law ought not to

[49] (340) *Senate Documents,* Twenty-fifth Congress, Third Session, No. 165.

[50] (310) *House Journal,* Twenty-fifth Congress, First Session, 53; September 14, 1837.

[51] (940) *Ibid.,* Thirty-fifth Congress, First Session, 199.

[52] February 16, 1860.

be made to vindicate the exemption of naturalized citizens of the United States from the claims of other governments of a right to enforce against such citizens the obligations of a prior and different allegiance.[53] Later the Judiciary Committee, at its own request, was discharged from the consideration of this last subject in the resolution, and it was referred to the Committee on Foreign Affairs.[54] A bill introduced by I. N. Morris,

to provide for expatriation, etc., and to restrain citizens of the United States from entering into the military or naval service of foreign States, etc., and for other purposes,

was before the House Judiciary Committee in 1860; and was ordered printed, together with certain notes on the subject, in March of that year. A few days later, on motion of its chairman, the committee was discharged from further consideration of this bill.[55]

[53] (1041) *House Journal,* Thirty-sixth Congress, First Session, 314.

[54] (1042) *ibid.,* 994.

[55] (1041) *ibid.,* 216, 311, 423, 519.

CHAPTER X

THE ACT OF 1824

After the War of 1812, and with the coming of peace to Europe, immigration to the United States increased very rapidly. It was generally welcomed until 1838. Nearly all of the agitation on the subject of naturalization had for its object the removal of restrictions upon aliens. The provision of the laws that required a previous declaration of intention was the one most vigorously attacked. The opposition to it was successful in changing the law in several respects during the decade from 1820 to 1830. The general principle that there should be a preliminary testing period under a declaration of intention withstood all attacks upon it, but the period required was reduced from three to two years. A special modification of the law was made in favor of aliens who came to the United States as minors, and hence were incapable of taking the steps preliminary to citizenship during the early years of their residence. It was thought that persons who cast their lot with the United States in youth could more safely be trusted to make good citizens than those who came

167

later. Their admission did not require the same safeguards. Another change was in the interest of persons whose long residence in the United States might compensate for the lack of the required declaration. The history of these measures is now to be considered. The first two of the changes mentioned above were made by the act of 1824, and the third by that of 1828.

Early in 1822, on motion of Tucker (S. C.), the House Judiciary Committee considered the matter of allowing aliens who had resided in the United States one year before the beginning of the War of 1812, and continuously since, to become citizens without complying with the requirement of a declaration of intention three years before their application. The report on the subject was as follows:

> The condition is, in the opinion of the committee, a very reasonable one, and one with which it is easy to comply where the intention really exists. To dispense with it is to commit a breach in the established system, and to make residence without declared intention to become a citizen, sufficient to entitle a person to become a citizen. This does not seem to the committee to be necessary or expedient, and they therefore offer the following resolution: *"Resolved, That the committee be discharged from the further consideration of the subject."*

The report and the subject were both effectually disposed of for that session by reference to the Committee of the Whole House on the State of the Union.[1] The next session the House ordered the report to be reprinted.[2]

Preliminary to the passage of the act of 1824 there was consideration of a request for a private naturalization act, the object of which was to avoid the requirement of residence after a declaration of intention. Representative Cobb (Ga.) presented the petition of Peter L. Jackson, representing that he was a native of England, and came to the United States while a minor in 1802. He had not been naturalized, but had grown to manhood in the country, had married a native American woman, raised a family of children, and had repeatedly performed military duty in the last war with England. Since the war he had repeatedly been appointed to office by the executive and the people of Georgia, and had ever considered himself to be a citizen of the United States. Recently, however, he had been ejected from a civil office to which he had been elected, as the result of a judicial decision that he was not a citizen of the United States. He prayed that a special act might be passed admitting him forthwith to the rights

---

[1] (62) *House Journal,* Seventeenth Congress, First Session, 268, 349; (70) *House Reports of Committees,* Seventeenth Congress, First Session, No. 68.

[2] (86) *House Reports of Committees,* Seventeenth Congress, Second Session, No. 47.

of a citizen. The House Judiciary Committee, to whom this petition was referred, reported briefly: "Resolved, That the prayer of the petitioner ought not to be granted." The House concurred in the report.[3] Probably no favor would have been shown to any proposition to naturalize a single individual. The same session of Congress that rejected this petition, did, however, let the bars down for the class of persons to which this petitioner belonged.

The aliens of Paterson, N. J., at a meeting held October 21, 1823, perhaps inaugurated the movement leading to the changes that were made in 1824. They addressed "their fellow emigrants throughout the union," and called on all brother-aliens to co-operate with them. They said:

We, conceiving that the alien laws are detrimental to the United States, and injurious to us, deem it to be our duty to make an appeal to Congress to obtain a revision of them.

They were unalterably convinced that their full participation in the republican immunities was essentially interwoven with the prosperity of the commonwealth. The interest of the citizen and the republican immigrant were in union of sentiment. They hoped that discus-

[3] (92) *House Journal*, Eighteenth Congress, First Session, 86, 118.

sion of the subject of intention would make
clear that the probationary laws were opposite in their nature to the liberal and mild institutions of the United States, which had at-
tracted them from transatlantic despotism.
Thousands of them, unacquainted with the
nature of the existing alien law, had neglected
to comply with its provisions. They had
lacked knowledge of the proper mode of procedure, and distance from the proper authorities had been an almost insuperable obstacle
in their way. They called earnestly for the
attention of their brother-aliens to consider
their best interests, and submitted to them
the propriety of petitioning Congress to facilitate the right of citizenship. They urged the
aliens in each state to solicit the aid of their
members of Congress. They appealed to citizens also for assistance to obtain their reasonable request. It would remove the prejudices
generated by national feeling, and enable the
firm supporters of the government to distinguish friends from foes. Finally, they resolved
to raise a subscription to further their views,
and solicited editors generally to insert their
appeal.[4]

Petitions from various parts of the country
were soon before Congress. New Jersey and

[4] *Niles Register,* XXV, 150.

New York City were represented, and citizens of New York supported the request of the aliens in a separate petition.[5] Sundry aliens of Louisiana prayed that the laws upon the subject of naturalization be amended to the end that greater facilities might be afforded to foreigners intending to become citizens. Other Louisiana aliens prayed that a special law might be passed for their naturalization, for reasons set forth in their petition.[6] A memorial of certain inhabitants of Savannah, Ga., represented that they were natives of foreign countries, who had reported, upon their arrival in America, to the clerks of courts of the United States and signed a declaration of intention to become citizens of the United States. They had also taken the oaths, and ever since, until lately, had supposed themselves to be citizens of the United States. A recent decision of the United States District Court for Georgia had held that their naturalizations were illegal, and that they were aliens in consequence of their not having reported themselves and signed the declaration in open court. They prayed that one act might be passed to legalize the acts by which it was supposed that they became citizens.[7]

[5] *Annals of Congress,* Eighteenth Congress, First Session, 1428; January 19, February 9, 1824.

[6] *House Journal,* Eighteenth Congress, First Session, 238, 288.

[7] *Annals of Congress,* Eighteenth Congress, First Session, 1619; February 23, 1824.

The House referred the Louisiana petitions to a select committee,[8] and a little later transferred to it a number of petitions that had gone to the Judiciary Committee.[9] Among the subjects transferred to the special committee was a resolution of inquiry as to whether any changes were necessary in the existing naturalization laws,

and also, into the expediency of furnishing copies of those laws to the courts of the several states authorized to naturalize aliens, so as to secure to persons desirous of naturalization the benefit thereof.[10]

As a rule, reference to a select committee meant consignment to the hands of friends. It was the regular method of saving a measure from a hostile standing committee, or from a committee whose attitude toward it might be uncertain. A bill was reported in part on March 8.[11] Apparently the committee intended to deal with the variety of questions involved in the various petitions before it, but for some reason, probably because the Senate was making progress with a measure before it, the House carried its own measures no farther.

[8] February 16, and March 3.

[9] (92) *House Journal*, Eighteenth Congress, First Session, 238, 288; *Annals of Congress*, Eighteenth Congress, First Session, 1627; February 24, 1824.

[10] (92) *House Journal*, Eighteenth Congress, First Session, 46.

[11] (92) *ibid.*, 298.

The Senate had started from a petition of Indiana aliens, praying for a modification of the laws. The first bill reported by its Judiciary Committee was recommitted. It was reported back without amendment and laid on the table, and a new bill that accompanied it was pushed rapidly to its passage, after undergoing one amendment, on the motion of Holmes (Me.), limiting its provisions to free white persons. A motion by Taylor (Va.) to strike out all after the first section, and insert two new sections, was lost. Nothing can be conjectured as to the nature and purpose of this amendment.[12]

There remained only six days of the session. After three days the House Judiciary Committee reported the Senate bill without amendment. The House passed it the next day at an evening session, and the President signed it the same night.[13]

Meanwhile the House Judiciary Committee had received instructions to inquire into the expediency "of fixing, by law, the fees proper to be allowed for the official duties performed in relation to the naturalization of aliens," [14]

[12] (88) *Senate Journal,* Eighteenth Congress, First Session, 136, 151, 196, 290, 298, 449, 455; *Annals of Congress,* Eighteenth Congress, First Session, May 21, 1824.

[13] (92) *House Journal,* Eighteenth Congress, First Session, 568, 569, 577, 593; (88) *Senate Journal,* Eighteenth Congress, First Session, 499.

[14] March 3, 1824.

and the expediency "of prohibiting, by law,
the employment of any person, except a citizen of the United States, in any of the Depart-
ments of the Government." [15]

The act of 1824 was entitled: "An act in
further addition to 'An act to establish an
uniform rule of naturalization, and to repeal
the acts heretofore passed.'" Sec. 1 provided
that any alien, being free white and under
twenty-one, who should have resided in the
United States three years, and continued to
reside therein to the time of making his application to become a citizen, might, after becoming twenty-one, and after he had resided
in the United States five years, including three
years of his minority, be admitted a citizen of
the United States without having made the
required declaration three years before his admission. The required declaration was to be
made at the time of his admission, and also
the further declaration on oath, and proof to
the satisfaction of the court, that for the previous three years it had been his bona fide intention to become a citizen of the United
States. In all other respects the former laws
were to be complied with.

Sec. 2 declared that no certificates of naturalization previously obtained from any court

[15] March 8, 1824; (92) *House Journal*, Eighteenth Congress,
First Session, 289, 299.

of record should be deemed invalid in consequence of omission to comply with the requirements of sec. 1 of the act of 1816. Sec. 3
referred to any declarations of intention made
bona fide before the clerks of proper courts,
and made them as valid as though they had
been made before the courts themselves. The
final section provided that a declaration of intention to become a citizen made according
to law by any free white alien, two years before his admission, should be a sufficient compliance with the requirement of the law.[16]

Aliens still urged further modifications of
the laws for naturalization. Van Buren presented a petition to this effect in 1825, and
another in 1826.[17] In 1826, on the motion of
Weems (Md.), the House Committee on
Judiciary was instructed to consider the expediency of amending the naturalization laws
so that when any person applied for citizenship and proved, by two witnesses, five years'
previous residence in the United States, with
the places of the same, he should be deemed
a citizen and be entitled to a certificate of naturalization, although he had omitted, from
ignorance or improper information, or from
being a minor, to have entered his name as a

[16] *Statutes at Large,* IV, 69.

[17] *Niles Register,* XXVII, 412; (124) *Senate Journal,* Nineteenth Congress, First Session, 103.

candidate for naturalization. The committee
was to inquire also as to other alterations that
might be necessary. Nothing came of this motion, and it was renewed the following session
with as little result.[18]

John Quincy Adams, then president, wrote
in his diary, July 3, 1827:

> Mr. Rush called, and read me a letter from himself to
> C. J. Ingersoll upon the subject of naturalizing foreigners.
> He is averse to all laws restrictive of naturalization, and
> would confer the rights of a native citizen to every for-
> eigner from the day of his setting foot upon our soil. With
> this opinion I do not exactly concur.[19]

A year later [20] the above-mentioned committee received similar instructions as to "revising and reducing into one, the several acts
of Congress establishing rules of naturalization;" and, also, as to admitting aliens who
were in the United States before 1812 on the
same terms as those who arrived before 1802
were admitted (i. e., without a previous declaration of intention). For the third time
Weems now secured the reference of a resolution for inquiry as to amending the naturalization laws.[21] His former resolutions had contemplated the admission of aliens, although

[18] (130) *House Journal*, Nineteenth Congress, First Session,
347; (147) *House Journal*, Nineteenth Congress, Second Session,
87.

[19] *Memoirs*, VII, 301.

[20] December 11, 1827.   [21] December 20, 1827.

they had omitted to make declaration of intention. The instructions mentioned had now provided for the consideration of a part of that subject. Weems' motion directed the inquiry into the expediency "of so harmonizing the several conflicting laws" on the subject of naturalization "that persons heretofore or hereafter applying to become citizens of the United States," upon making the required proofs of five years' previous residence, should, two years thereafter, be deemed citizens of the United States, and, upon taking the oath of allegiance and paying the legal costs, should be entitled to receive certificates of naturalization.[22] This seems to involve giving the rights of citizenship without the requirement of an oath of allegiance, and without the expense involved in procuring a certificate. Perhaps it was thought that the oath need not be required, nor would a certificate be necessary while the new citizen remained in the United States. If, however, he wished the certificate for any purpose, let him take the oath of allegiance and pay for the certificate. The oath of allegiance would thus become merely a special pledge of allegiance already due.

A little later,[23] Buchanan reported from the Judiciary Committee a bill to amend the nat-

[22] (168) *House Journal*, Twentieth Congress, First Session, 76.
[23] January 30, 1828.

uralization acts. In a statement to the House concerning the matter, he said that an alien must prove five years' residence in the United States by disinterested testimony, and must exhibit a certificate that he had declared his intention two years before he made application to become a citizen. Neither of those provisions was to be interfered with. A certificate of registry before a court was also required as the only legal evidence of the time of arrival in the United States. An alien who had lived in the United States ten years must reside therein five years longer, if he had neglected to register his arrival. Such neglect was common, indeed almost universal. The law was either unknown by them or was neglected. Some courts carried out the requirement of the law, while others did not do so. In 1824 Congress had made certificates of naturalization good without their reciting the fact of registry. The committee thought that it would simplify the law to dispense with the registry. Sec. 2 was to provide for another class of cases. Aliens who had arrived since the passage of the act of 1802 must show a certificate of declaration of intention made two years before their application for admission. The committee thought that this might be dispensed with, if they showed continuous residence in the United States from before June 18, 1812. This would require proof of constant residence for nearly sixteen years, and accorded strictly with former precedents. Similar provisions had been inserted in the law in 1802 and in 1804, but none since then for twenty-four years. In thus representing the matter, Buchanan ignored the fact that the chief object of the former provisions was to mitigate special hardships arising from changes made in the laws. The bill passed both houses without any amendment,[24] and became a law May 24, 1828.[25]

In 1835 the House had before it a memorial of sundry citizens of New York state praying that the naturalization law be so amended that thereafter no declaration of intention should be required, but that aliens should be fully entitled to all the privileges of citizenship, if they proved two years' residence in the United States. The Judiciary Committee, to which this was referred, was soon thereafter discharged from further consideration of it, and the petition was laid on the table.[26]

[24] In the House a paper containing amendments that he intended to propose to the bill was submitted by Verplank (N. Y.) and referred to the committee of the whole in charge of the bill. This was on February 15.

[25] (168) *House Journal,* Twentieth Congress, First Session, 233, 662, 670, 677, 875; (162) *Senate Journal,* Twentieth Congress, First Session, 352, 353, 427, 484; *Register of Debates,* Twentieth Congress, First Session. 2555.

[26] (270) *House Journal,* Twenty-third Congress, Second Session, 307, 358.

In the early thirties the House Judiciary
Committee was three times instructed to inquire into the expediency of putting into a
single act all of the naturalization provisions
then in force.   Twice these instructions included also the question of revising the laws.
A bill was reported in February, 1832, making
further provision for the naturalization of
aliens.[27]   Nothing came of any of these measures.

Several measures giving or seeking to give
additional civil rights to aliens may be noticed
here.   One of them was passed in 1832, as
the result of an inquiry relative to amending
the patent law "so as to place aliens who have
applied to become citizens on an equal footing with citizens, or aliens who have resided
two years in the United States." [28]   Taylor, who
reported the bill, said that the Patent Act of
1790 gave aliens the same privileges as citizens; that of 1793 had limited the privileges
to citizens; that of 1800 had extended them
to aliens two years in the United States, who
made oath that their invention had not been
made anywhere before.   At least seventeen

[27] (205) *loc. cit.*, Twenty-first Congress, Second Session, 60, 171;
(215) *Ibid.*, Twenty-second Congress, First Session, 57, 317; (232)
Ibid., Twenty-second Congress, Second Session, 48.

[28] (205) *ibid.*, Twenty-first Congress, Second Session, 258;
(215) *ibid.*, Twenty-second Congress, First Session, 158, 177, 1145,
1148, 1187.

acts had been passed since, dispensing with the two years' residence, and requiring only actual residence at the time of the application for a patent. The bill in hand was on the principle of those seventeen acts. It required residence in the United States, declaration of intention to become a citizen, and the oath of the act of 1800.[29] Besides the points mentioned by Taylor, the act provided that rights granted under it should lapse, if the invention were not in use within one year and continuously thereafter, and also in case the inventor failed to become a citizen at the earliest legal period.[30] In 1837 there was a proposal to amend the laws in relation to imprisonment for debt so as to place alien plaintiffs on the same footing as citizens as to legal remedies.[31] In 1840 the question of granting letters testamentary and administrative to aliens in the District of Columbia was referred to the House Judiciary Committee.[32] The New York Legislature in 1845 passed an act to allow John Horsley Palmer, president of the Bank of England, to hold real estate.[33] He was

[29] 12 *Register of Debates,* Twenty-first Congress, Second Session, 1500.

[30] *Statutes at Large,* IV, 577.

[31] (300) *House Journal,* Twenty-fourth Congress, Second Session, 320.

[32] (362) *ibid.,* Twenty-sixth Congress, First Session, 966.

[33] *Niles Register,* LXVIII, 179.

said to have been very favorable to investments in America, but of course he had no intention of becoming even an alien resident. Whether he could by the law of a western state have gained the right to purchase federal land therein, would be an interesting question.

CHAPTER XI

THE BEGINNINGS OF NATIVE AMERICANISM

There are no reliable statistics of immigration before 1820. The arrivals during Washington's administration were chiefly English and French. Transportation rates were high, and were kept up by legislation limiting the number of passengers to two per ton of the ship's capacity. The immigrant was necessarily a person of some means, and opposition to him was from a political, not an economic, point of view. The actual influence of the French Revolution upon immigration was very great, and its anticipated influence was much greater. With the advent of the Napoleonic period most of the immigration ceased. It began again in greater numbers, and from other countries also, when peace returned to Europe. We have seen that the inclination in America generally was for some time thereafter in favor of it. Every succeeding period of economic depression, however, produced a violent reaction against it.

The immigration during each of the two decades ending in 1820 and 1830 was about 1 per cent. of the total population at the end of the decade. During the next decade it reached 3½ per cent. of the population in 1840. This percentage was a little more than doubled during the next decade, and for succeeding periods it has been 8, 6, 6, and 8 per cent. The population, the base of these percentages, increased quite uniformly by one-third during all except the later periods.

Niles Register, during 1816, made frequent mention of the continuing immigration. During the following winter immigration was "powerful" and would increase.[1] In September, 1817, an article favoring immigration estimated the average at ten thousand per year. That year it would be thirty thousand.[2] The arrivals for one week in 1819 were given as 1,414. Then came the first note of disapproval, as follows: "The time has been when we were pleased to see the progress of emigration, it is now painful to observe it, because of the want of employment for our own people."[3] A few weeks later[4] the swelling tide of foreigners had aroused greater apprehensions, and the first fears of foreign paupers were expressed. "We have always until just now greeted the stranger on his arrival here with pleasure." There had been room for all,

---

[1] *Niles Register,* XI, 359.
[2] *Ibid.,* XIII, 35.
[3] *Ibid.,* July 31, 1819.
[4] September 18, 1819.

but the population in the maritime districts, and in some parts of the interior, seemed too dense. The western country was overstocked by the domestic emigration. A good many from England, disappointed in finding employment, were on their way home.

It is reported, that to relieve themselves of their paupers, many such will be sent to the United States by the church wardens, etc., of England! It will therefore become the state authorities to be careful to take the proper securities of those who bring passengers, that they will not become chargeable on the public.

Probably not fewer than four thousand persons had arrived in two weeks, and perhaps a thousand more in a month by way of Canada. The writer felt sure that forty thousand was more than had ever arrived in any one year, and that never had so many come any former year as that year. Yet, he said, the New York Gazette spoke of an estimate by a gentleman of 500,000 in five years as what the emigration would amount to.[5] A week later it was said that perhaps three thousand had arrived the past week. This number was termed "enormous." [6]

In 1821 the editor thought: "It is not probable that 20,000 persons ever emigrated to the United States in any one year." [7] In 1822

[5] *Niles Register,* XVII, 38.
[6] *Ibid.,* 63.   [7] *Ibid.,* XX, 193.

many more had arrived than during the last
year. "They appeared to be substantial people." [8] At the close of the year the arrivals
had been greatly overestimated. They appeared, from the official statement laid before
Congress, to have been only 8,482 the past
year. Also this number included citizens of
the United States returning from foreign
ports, but did not include those arriving by
way of the St. Lawrence.[9] Late in 1823 Niles
ventured the opinion that the United States
in 1821 and 1822 "gained less than 6,000 persons from foreign places." [10] The same year
he noted that twenty-six paupers had been
sent over by a parish in Sussex, which had
paid their passage and given them some
money.[11] In 1827 it was noted that unusual
numbers were arriving, of classes "mostly not
such as we would generally prefer." [12] A year
later a large number of English families had
arrived lately at the expense of their parishes.
The significant comment followed: "there is
room enough for the poor people and ourselves." [13]

By the summer of 1831 the sentiment of
sympathy for paupers was fast going. Niles

[8] *Ibid.*, XXII, 155.   [9] *Ibid.*, XXIII, 305.
[10] *Ibid.*, XXV, 232. He probably means each year.
[11] *Ibid.*, XXIV, 113.
[12] *Ibid.*, XXXII, 310.   [13] *Ibid.*, XXXIV, 411.

indorsed a Massachusetts law to allow no
alien to land till the master of the vessel on
which he came had paid the city five dollars.
He would not check desirable immigration
but concluded that the country was "wretched-
ly imposed upon." The British were deluging
their cities with paupers, and this required a
strong corrective.[14] Again, immigration was
very large. "The greater number of them are
men of substance and character." "Some car-
goes of English paupers are expected."[15] A
little later there is a statement that all the
cities are severely taxed to care for foreign
paupers. Nearly half of the inmates of the
New York almshouse were foreigners. Strong
regulations should be adopted. "Let those
who suck the orange not throw the peel at
us."[16] Again (September 15, 1832), there
was much greater immigration than ever before—100,000 or more already that year. Very
many Germans were arriving at Philadelphia
and Baltimore. They were hardy, healthy,
and industrious, and nearly all of them had
the means of going to the interior. They
would soon be among their most valuable citizens. They differed much from the loads of
English paupers "shoveled upon us." They

[14] *Loc. cit.*, XL, 74, 130.
[15] *Ibid.*, 273; June 18, 1831.   [16] *Ibid.*, XLI, 356.

would work and support themselves, and not fill the poorhouses.[17]

In 1833 there appeared a memorial of the mayor and council of Baltimore to the general assembly, calling for relief from the influx of foreign paupers. All reports of the health officers since 1827 had called attention to the destitute and diseased condition of emigrants. They were filling the almshouse, and swarms of foreign beggars were infesting the streets. While they would extend the right hand to every immigrant able and willing to support himself, they requested laws to protect them from others.[18] A little later Niles noted that a late law "may abate this nuisance." An unprecedented number of immigrants from Germany were expected, sober and industrious, exactly the kind needed.[19] Again (June 8, 1833), immigrants were pouring in from Ireland, England, Scotland, and Wales; but the greater number, most probably, were from Germany. Many were of the best productive classes, while others were mere day laborers. They were patient and industrious, and exceedingly economical.[20]

As the country was passing through a most prosperous period, Niles recovered from his fears. In 1833, he wrote:

[17] *Ibid.*, XLIII, 40.
[18] *Ibid.*, 391.
[19] *Ibid.*, XLIV, 131.
[20] *Ibid.*, 233.

There can not be a want of it [room] for some hundred years to come; and for the sake of the human race it is earnestly to be wished that the United States of America should have first rank among the nations of the earth, and remain "an asylum for the oppressed," the hope and pride of all men who love liberty.[21]

Six months later there was "a great surplus of labor just now," and he did "not wish new importations to send our own people supperless to bed." [22] "We regret to see that many emigrants are arriving from Europe . . . We are already much overstocked with laborers." Foreign paupers were discharged on their shores. It seemed reasonable to expect that the United States and Canada would receive one hundred thousand immigrants in 1834. Many of the Germans were well provided for, "though we had several shipments of disgusting paupers or beggars from Germany, a year or two ago." [23]

The foregoing ideas and extracts from one of the most intelligently edited papers cast much light upon the problem of immigration. They exhibit influences and tendencies the existence of which at that time has not been generally recognized. In connection with them the rapid increase of immigration thereafter, the changes in its character, and the

21 *Loc. cit.*, XLV, 2.
22 *Ibid.*, XLVI, 1.   23 *Ibid.*, 218, 244, 398.

deterioration in its quality go far to explain the outbreak of Native-Americanism and Know-Nothingism, whose influence upon naturalization I am about to trace.

The Native American Association organized on a distinctly political basis at a meeting held in Washington on July 11, 1837, in the midst of the panic conditions of that year. The meeting was described as large, and composed of Native Americans of all parties. An address set forth the necessity for a repeal of the naturalization law, to save their institutions from the corruption of foreign countries and themselves from the loss of their birthright. A preamble and constitution were unanimously adopted. The former declared that all governments were bound by the principles of national preservation to govern by their own citizens. The republican form of government of the United States was believed to be an object of fear and dislike to the advocates of monarchy in Europe. The United States were imperatively called upon to administer their peculiar system free from all foreign influence. By admitting strangers they were weakening the attachments of natives, and could gain only a sordid allegiance from foreigners. They were maintaining in its most extended form the right of the native-born American. He only should exercise the duties of government, from the highest to the lowest post. To that end they said: "We shall advocate the entire repeal of the naturalization law by congress." As the constitution forbade *ex post facto* action, they sought only prospective action. They solemnly believed that Americans should unite as brothers. A critical period had been reached, when every wind blew ragged paupers to their cities, and brought elements of degradation and disorder. A great moral revolution was to be fought.

The Constitution bound members to cooperate to procure the repeal of the naturalization laws by all lawful means; not to hold guiltless the man who should place foreigners in office; and declared that they would be a separate and independent party of Native Americans, and would not connect themselves to any religious sect or denomination. Resolutions were adopted to the effect that they would seek to support a Native American press in Washington, and would prepare an appeal to the Native Americans of the United States.

At a later meeting [24] a memorial to Congress was unanimously adopted. It was de-

[24] December 26, 1837.

scribed as the memorial of more than nine hundred citizens of the United States associated at Washington under the name of the Native American Association.   It urged that the power to naturalize was given to Congress to add to the physical strength of the United States, attract skilled workmen, and draw capital thither.   It had not been anticipated that it would be used so as to place "a large portion of the power of this government in the hands of adventurers of every clime," before they learned the language, or the first principles of a republican government.   The very short term of five years would not qualify a foreigner for citizenship.   There was manifold injustice and soon to be serious danger in giving them such privileges.   Already many of the most important elections had been swayed and decided by the votes of foreigners, notoriously ignorant, used by artful demagogues.   Rome had lost her liberties by admitting large bands of foreigners, and England had preserved hers by excluding them.   They humbly believed that the fit time had arrived when the laws should be carefully revised and amended, or altogether repealed.

A strong plea was made against pauper and criminal immigrants.   The governments of Europe, seeking to free themselves from a vast increase of pauperism and crime, had chosen the free and happy American land for their criminal and burdensome classes. Any wish to shut doors against reputable immigrants was disclaimed. They desired the land to continue for all time, in a fair and proper sense, "an asylum for the oppressed of all nations." To worthy foreigners they would say: "Come to us and be at rest;" mingle not in politics; be content to be governed, and seek not to govern those who entertain you and give you shelter and protection; exercise freely every religious and social right, but do not expect political privileges, at least until length of residence has guaranteed you to be fully acquainted with the nature and extent of the obligations of American citizens.

In conclusion they prayed Congress to repeal the naturalization laws, or so modify them as best to secure to native citizens the full enjoyment of the privileges and rights they were entitled to under the Constitution; and also to make ample provision for the protection of the United States from any future influx of foreign paupers and convicts.

Patton, who presented the memorial,[25] moved its reference to a select committee and accepted instructions to the committee, moved

[25] January 8, 1838.

by Lincoln, to consider the expediency of revising and amending the laws so as to require a longer term of residence in the United States previous to the admission of foreigners to citizenship, and greater checks and securities against frauds in the means and process of obtaining naturalization; also legislation regarding vagrants and paupers sent to the United States. Debate arose on the question of reference, the opposition seeking to send it to the Committee on Judiciary; and it was laid on the table to take its turn under the rules.[26] Hopeless, apparently, of securing a select committee, although soon after a less imposing memorial was referred to one, Lincoln at length moved to instruct the Judiciary Committee as above, and it was done.[27]

A memorial of over five hundred citizens of two towns of Massachusetts urged an inquiry to solve four questions: (1) whether there were designs against the liberties of the country by means of an influx of foreign immigration; (2) whether the character of the immigration did not augur a vast increase of pauperism and crime in the land; (3) whether oaths of allegiance were not binding some to

[26] (320) *House Journal,* Twenty-fifth Congress, Second Session, 235; (325) *House Executive Documents,* Twenty-fifth Congress, Second Session, V, No. 98.

[27] (320) *House Journal,* Twenty-fifth Congress, Second Session, 465.

a foreign despotic prince, and whether such had equal claims upon the government with dutiful subjects, or were entitled to the confidence of the nation; (4) whether there was not a foreign conspiracy against the government, and measures and plans working for its execution. They entreated that a faithful investigation be made and action taken.[28]

A few weeks later the subject was again brought before Congress in the memorial of ninety-seven electors of Washington County, N. Y., praying a revision of the laws regulating the naturalization of foreigners. It declared that the easy access of foreigners of doubtful morals and hostile political principles to the elective franchise was a source of danger to the country's civil and religious liberties. The Constitution had not contemplated a majority hostile to its principles. Since naturalization laws had been thought to be necessary, let them be adequate to their defense. They had deep concern at the influx of Catholics, but sought legislative defense only against the political principles interwoven with their religion. They desired inquiry as to whether a plan was not in operation for the subversion of their liberties by gaining American suffrage for Catholics from Europe; and whether

[28] *House Executive Documents,* Twenty-fifth Congress, Second Session, II, No. 70.

an amendment of the naturalization laws could more fully secure American institutions, liberties, etc., against the danger of subversion by foreign influence, and despotic tyrannical principles even under the cloak of religion. Here were Know-Nothing principles in full bloom, with foreigners and Catholics both to be feared. This time reference to a special committee was secured without any apparent opposition, and, later, various other papers, including that of the Native American Association, were referred to the same committee.[29]

Among these later papers was a memorial from citizens of New York City. The great and rapidly increasing influx of foreigners, the character and condition of a large proportion of them, the indiscriminate freedom by which suffrage was given them, they urged, were evils which wrongfully deprived "us" of "our" native rights, and fearfully tended to the destruction of their government and their liberties. They referred to "grievous frauds" in the execution of the Naturalization Law, and to paupers and criminals oppressing and de-

[29] The committee consisted of Russell (N. Y.), Lincoln (Mass.), Beatty (Ky.), Casey (Ill.), and Jackson (Mass.). Jackson soon after was excused, and Rhett (S. C.) took his place. (320) *House Journal,* Twenty-fifth Congress, Second Session, 576, 614; (327) *House Executive Documents,* Twenty-fifth Congress, Second Session, VII, No. 154.

moralizing. The time for naturalization was quite too short. They earnestly prayed an amendment requiring twenty-one years' residence of all aliens not already having declared intentions, before they should be entitled to the suffrage. If guilty of crime that would disqualify a native, even that residence should not qualify them. The power to grant certificates of naturalization should be confined to Congress, the Supreme Court, and the superior courts of the states.[30] This was, perhaps, the first mention of the twenty-one years' residence period in a document that reached Congress.

Some time before this agitation began, the report of a legislative committee of Louisiana had shown a 50 per cent. increase of patients in the charity hospital of New Orleans coincident with unprecedented good health in the city. Of nearly six thousand inmates, nearly 70 per cent. had been aliens. The *Baltimore American* had reported that among the inmates of the almshouses of Boston, New York, Philadelphia, and Baltimore, in all over ten thousand, there were 10 per cent. more foreigners than Americans. These reports related to the year 1835. In 1837 the mayor of New York, allowed by state law to collect

[30] (329) *House Executive Documents,* Twenty-fifth Congress, Second Session, IX, No. 313.

from one to ten dollars as commutation money in place of taking from masters of vessels an indemnity bond to secure the city from foreign paupers, decided to collect ten dollars per passenger instead of the one dollar before collected.[31]

The report of the Select Committee on Foreign Paupers and Naturalization laws [32] contained 116 pages, and included a report from the secretary of state and one from the secretary of the treasury. It referred to simultaneous appeals to Congress from different sections to save the country from the blighting influence of a pauper, vagrant, and malefactor population sent over at the expense of foreign governments, arriving destitute, and becoming at once burdensome. One-half of the pauper population of the United States and three-fourths of the convicts in Sing Sing were foreign. The foreign population of the United States was about one in nineteen. Foreign influence was most dangerous to governments, and the influence of the Old World monarchies was especially so to the United States. The idea that foreigners on their arrival were entitled to the privileges of citizenship was not well founded. Some were worthy, but no rule of discrimination could be adopted without

[31] *Niles Register*, XLIX, 62, 69; LII, 250.
[32] July 2, 1838.

creating invidious distinctions. The committee concluded that the term of probation should be extended from five years to ——————— years. Owing to great complaint of frauds in the lower courts, and in order to preserve uniformity in the execution of the laws, naturalization should be confined to the courts of the United States or to the supreme court in the states. Record of the previous declaration of intention was also thought advisable.

An appendix contained reports from American consuls in regard to the deportation of paupers from Europe. Passage from Bremen was as low as sixteen dollars. Hamburg had deported condemned criminals to New York. Some Irish landholders, where tenants were becoming too numerous, had sent from Dublin perhaps a hundred a year for five or six years. From Liverpool and London it was reported that some parishes sent abroad their excess population, always giving from five to ten pounds in money besides passage and food. Convicts, workhouse inmates, the old and decrepit, were never sent. Six hundred were sent from Liverpool in 1830 by parishes, five hundred in 1832, and not more than three hundred in any year since. In 1831 complaint had been made to England of an act of the Jamaica government under which American vessels touching at that island had been compelled to carry away a number of paupers proportioned to the size of the vessel.[33]

The committee, after obtaining permission, introduced two bills, which after some debate, were sent to the Committee of the Whole on the State of the Union.[34] One member of the special committee, Beatty, asked for time that he might submit a counter report. He protested against the monstrous doctrine in the report, reviving in full force the doctrines of 1798.

Late in the following session of Congress, the House referred to the committee of the whole "to which is committed the bill reported last session" a memorial "signed, it is believed, by several thousand citizens of the state of Louisiana."[35] They asserted that hundreds of foreigners, alien to the obligations they so readily incurred, were daily acquiring rights. Both parties, throughout the United States, made constant charge of bribery of foreigners in elections and this was imperiling the welfare of the country. The existing facilities for naturalization were

---

[33] (336) *House Reports of Committees,* Twenty-fifth Congress, Second Session, II, No. 70.

[34] (320) *House Journal,* 1207; *Congressional Globe,* 489; July 2, 1838.

[35] *Congressional Globe,* Twenty-fifth Congress, Third Session, 178; February 7, 1839.

highly injurious to the safety and perpetuity of free institutions. A dreadful deterioration of morals and increase of crime were apparent within ten or fifteen years. Seven hundred convicts had been sent out from one place. The whole country was suffering. They would not abridge the rights of those naturalized or who had declared intentions, but they wished the passage of a law putting native-born and naturalized citizens at least on an equal footing.[36] They solicited the entire repeal of the naturalization acts then in force, and ample provision for the protection of the United States from the indiscriminate influx of foreign emigrants. Should these things be delayed, ere long they would have to sue at the footstool of a power alien in feelings, prejudices, and aspirations.[37]

The Twenty-Fifth Congress expired without further action on these subjects. There was, however, a resolution introduced looking to the exclusion from the privileges of citizenship of the children of persons who removed from the United States and took the oath of allegiance to the government in which they resided, until they should become

[36] This is doubtless a plea for twenty-one years' residence before naturalization, and indicates that the argument for it had been developed.

[37] (347) *House Executive Documents,* Twenty-fifth Congress, Third Session, IV, No. 162.

naturalized like other foreigners. Debate arose upon this, and it was laid over under the rules, not to appear again.[38]

During 1840 much attention was given in and out of Congress to the naturalization question, and a strong effort was made in both the Senate and the House to repeal the existing laws. In the House easier naturalization was sought; in the Senate, more stringent legislation. The matter was more quiet the following year, and in 1842 there might seem the indication of a reaction in a proposition debated briefly in the Senate to return to the two-year requirement of the act of 1790. In 1843, however, the twenty-one-year agitation became distinctly aggressive. Thereafter, until the Civil War, it had to be reckoned with continuously as an important political factor. Sometimes, in various eastern states, the issue involved in it dominated all other issues.

Two letters written in 1840 by the Whig candidate for president give an indication of the political importance already attached to the question of naturalization. The first was written [39] to a committee in Indiana. It acknowledged the receipt of a letter mention-

[38] (343) *House Journal,* Twenty-fifth Congress, Third Session, 398; January 28, 1839.

[39] July 4, 1840.

ing a report prevailing "that I am averse to emigrants from foreign countries being naturalized short of twenty years," and declared that he had never ceased to pronounce this a calumny. On the contrary, he had done everything in his power to facilitate the acquisition of citizenship by those near him; and, when in Congress, to give them before their naturalization the same privileges in taking up and holding public lands as natives.[40] In the other letter he wrote to a Philadelphian:

Through the whole course of my political life, I am satisfied, that no sentence ever fell from my lips, which could be construed into an unfriendly feeling to the Europeans who have emigrated hither, to enjoy the advantages which our free institutions afford, or a wish to extend the period, which is fixed by the existing laws, for their full admission to the rights of citizenship.[41]

A petition from Louisiana, in form at least the same as that before the House in the previous Congress, was referred to the Senate Judiciary Committee early in 1840.[42] It sought the entire repeal of the naturalization laws, and new stringent legislation on the subject. The committee reported that the prayer of the petitioners ought not to be

[40] *Niles Register,* LVIII, 397.
[41] *North American Review,* LII, 220; January, 1841.
[42] January 7.

granted.[43] Two other petitions for the repeal of the naturalization laws, one of these
from citizens of Louisiana and the other, presented by Clay, from citizens of the United
States engaged in the navigation of the western waters, were laid on the table. The Senate adopted the report of its committee.[44]

At the same session the Senate passed a
joint resolution for the printing of all the naturalization laws "as soon as practicable," but it
seems not to have passed the House.[45] Meanwhile, in the House, Hand (N. Y.) had obtained leave and introduced a bill to establish a uniform rule of naturalization, and to
repeal all existing acts on that subject. A
controversy ensued as to its reference, but
it went to the Judiciary Committee and remained there.[46] Early in the following session
Hand again got leave and presented a similar bill. This time he pressed the question of
reference to a vote, and lost by a narrow majority. He wished to send it to the Committee of the Whole House on the State of the
Union, where thus early in the session he

[43] February 12, 1840.

[44] February 18, 1840. (353) *Senate Journal*, Twenty-sixth
Congress, First Session, 81, 174, 179, 187, 208; (340) *Senate
Documents*, Twenty-fifth Congress, Third Session, III, No. 246.

[45] (353) *Senate Journal*, Twenty-sixth Congress, First Session,
330, 357, 363.

[46] (362) *House Journal*, Twenty-sixth Congress, First Session,
556, 587. See also *Congressional Globe*.

might expect to secure discussion upon it. On the other hand, it was argued that so important a subject should go to the Judiciary Committee. The vote was 96 to 90. Hand received practically the solid support of the Democratic party. John Quincy Adams wrote in his diary at the time that it was the second vote in which a sufficient number of the Kinderhook time-servers had given way to turn the majority.[47] A motion to reconsider the reference was debated at some length, but the debate is not reported. It was lost by a vote of 90 to 93,[48] and the bill was left to be buried by an unfavorable committee.

About the same time the Legislature of Missouri passed a memorial which was presented in the House and referred a year later.[49] This memorial referred to the existing excitement and discussion; to societies organized to procure the repeal of existing laws and the passage of a law extending the time of residence required for naturalization; and, finally, to the bill introduced in Congress by Hand to effect those pur-

[47] J. Q. Adams, *Memoirs*, X, 375.

[48] (381) *House Journal*, Twenty-sixth Congress, Second Session, 29, 42, 48, 59, 73. See also *Congressional Globe*.

[49] This memorial was approved February 16, 1841, and referred on January 7, 1842.

poses.[50] It declared that the objects of such societies are disapproved by the General Assembly of Missouri, "as being illiberal, intolerant in spirit, intending to rivet the bondage of mankind in the old world, and as unwise in effect, in repressing emigration to this country, and retarding its population and improvement." Senators were instructed and representatives requested to oppose the repeal of any law that provided for the naturalization of aliens, and to resist all measures designed to cause further delay or difficulty in the attainment of citizenship.[51] Nearly coincident with this action of the Missouri Legislature was the adoption by the Louisiana House of Representatives, by a vote of 25 to 10, of a resolution requesting that state's senators and representatives in Congress to endeavor to procure a change in the laws to require twenty-one years' consecutive residence in the United States for naturalization.[52]

In the committee of the whole in the House, during a debate on the Treasury-Note Bill, in January, 1841, Duncan (Ohio) exhibited a bill on the subject of naturalization

[50] This memorial shows a complete misconception of the character of Hand's bill.

[51] (402) *House Executive Documents,* Twenty-seventh Congress, Second Session, II, No. 37.

[52] *Niles Register,* LIX, 404.

that he intended to introduce, and explained that he expressed his views upon it then lest he should have no opportunity to introduce it. The object of the bill was to secure to those fleeing from despotism the rights and privileges that the ancestors of Americans secured by their flight. The elective franchise was the principal ingredient of free government. He had ever thought that the franchise as related to foreigners was unnecessarily limited and trammeled. Its difficulty and expense were incompatible with the nature of their free institutions. He had ever intended expressing his decided hostility to the naturalization laws as they existed, and trying to amend them in harmony with the nature of their government and the spirit of the Constitution. The government, at first an experiment, had been trammeled in some of its institutions. He would have it as free as the experience of the age would permit. There was no longer apology for restrictions, incompatible with their free institutions and personal rights, and originally founded in a lack of confidence in the people. He wished a shorter residence requirement, and naturalization with as little trouble and expense as possible. He would have the alien enjoy all the rights and privileges of the native-

born, not denied by the Constitution, upon
taking the oath of allegiance. Jefferson had
thought thus, and the Democratic party had
always favored the least possible restraint
upon naturalization and upon the suffrage. The
Federalists limited speech, debate, the press,
and the franchise. They "throw all the restrictions and embarrassments possible in
the way of naturalization," and are now en-
deavoring, in violation of the Constitution,
to deprive foreigners of the rights of citizenship. Proofs of his assertion were the act of
1798, passed by the Federalists and opposed
by the Democrats in Congress and out; the
act of 1802, opposed by the Federalists and
passed by the Democrats by the hardest effort. During the past winter, Hand, a Democrat, had early introduced a bill to shorten
the residence requirement. It was referred
to the Committee on Judiciary, a majority
of whom were Federalists or modern Whigs,
and "no power on earth was able to rescue
it from their hands. It slept the sleep of
death." A similar bill had been introduced
at the commencement of that session, and a
motion to refer it to a Committee of the
Whole House on the State of the Union
failed by a party vote. Reference to the Judiciary Committee carried by a party vote,

"every Federalist in the House voting for it and the Democracy against it, and there that bill now is safe for an eternal sleep." He could make a book of the party struggles on the subject of naturalization. The Federalists no longer stopped at restrictions and embarrassments, but sought to overthrow the privilege and constitutional rights of naturalization. They were seeking to make the foreigner a vassal.

Moreover, the country was overspread by Native American associations, whose object was shown by a petition from Illinois. It declared that time had "fulfilled the object had in view by our fathers" in giving Congress the power to naturalize foreigners, and that "farther admission of foreigners to a participation in the political rights of native Americans would be hurtful to the interests of our country." It would sooner or later prove destructive to their republican institutions. Attention was asked to petitions for repealing naturalization laws, and the entire repeal of such laws. In view of their object, these Federalist associations were infamous. In an address one of them has said:

We do solemnly resolve to oppose the election or appointment of any but American citizens to office, and henceforward use our united efforts and unsparing zeal to procure such an alteration in the naturalization laws as shall exclude from the right of suffrage all foreigners who come into the country after such law has passed.

Duncan declared further that Federalist opposition to foreigners was due to a preponderance of Germans and Irish among the immigrants, and to the fact that they were Democrats. The Federalists wished to abolish or prohibit the franchise of Irish and Germans because the latter were opposed to Federalist principles and institutions. He would maintain and extend their franchise because they favored democratic principles and institutions. The names of Lafayette, DeKalb, and Montgomery attested the obligation that was due to foreign blood poured out in the Revolution. The national jealousy and selfishness which shut out the foreigner rarely ever failed to produce evils. Good policy dictated admitting them. He closed with an appeal to foreigners to support democracy in order to secure to themselves the liberties which the Revolution had purchased.[53]

It was in August, 1842, that Walker in the Senate asked leave to bring in a bill "to reduce from five to two years the term of residence required for the naturalization of foreigners." This led to some discussion.

[53] *Congressional Globe,* Twenty-sixth Congress, Second Session, Appendix, 266; January, 1841.

Archer (Va.) declared that the subject was too grave to discuss at the heel of the session. He believed that naturalization laws were sufficient for all present purposes, and hoped that the Senate would resist the bill at the threshold. He moved to lay the request on the table. Walker replied that he was only seeking to revive the original act, sanctioned by Washington. Why should that be thought extraordinary! The aliens in 1830 had numbered 107,832. They were not counted in 1840; but if they had increased in proportion to the immigration, they numbered then 283,543. He objected entirely to the existence of so many aliens among the population, particularly as he did not believe they desired to be aliens. Increasing the number of aliens increased the jurisdiction of the federal courts. The vast immigration would increase the business of the Supreme Court prodigiously, and it was already so great that the court could do only one-half of its business at the last session. The debate in the McLeod case had called attention to the matter. Looking at what had taken place that very session in relation to cases in which aliens were parties, he was really alarmed at the enormous stretch of federal power. There was a necessity of diminishing the number of individuals in respect to whom the jurisdiction of the federal courts could be applied. If he had anticipated the possibility of any such objections as had been offered to the introduction of the bill, he might state other reasons more at length. He did not even then apprehend that the unusual course of refusing introduction to the bill would be taken. Every steamboat to the West was crowded with emigrants, going to purchase lands and place their families there. Their exclusion from citizenship had been so severely felt that two of the western states had given them the right to vote. This anomalous state of things was the result of changing the residence requirement from two to five years. There was no reason why men should not become citizens at the end of two as well as of five years. In case of war they had 300,000 aliens, mostly along the western frontier, who would be claimed by a foreign power. He rejoiced to see the numbers coming, welcomed them, and called attention to the efforts being put forth to divert them to the British colonies, and particularly to Australia, by granting the privilege of citizenship. Archer made answer that he was totally averse to other terms of naturalization. Their ancestors had soon changed from two to fourteen years, and then back to an intermediate term. Five years was a proper, just, and reasonable time. No good man ever renounced entirely his attachment to his native soil. Would it be proper in any sense to admit as citizens a large class having foreign attachments and feelings adverse to theirs? He desired to stigmatize the proposition by its immediate rejection. King thought courtesy alone might dictate a vote against Archer's motion. Walker's request was, however, laid on the table by a vote of 21 to 18.

CHAPTER XII

THE PERIOD OF AGGRESSIVE NATIVE AMERI-
CANISM

About forty petitions asking for amendment of the naturalization laws were received in both Senate and House during the
session of 1843-44. Some of them contained
hundreds of signatures. One was said to be
the petition of ten thousand citizens of New
York state.[1] One from Wisconsin Territory
sought an extension of the suffrage to residents of the territories.[2] Two from western
New York were in the interests of alien sailors whose employment took them out of the
territory of the United States during their
preliminary residence period.[3] Nearly all of
the others sought to extend the residence
period for naturalization to twenty-one years.

Buchanan presented one in the Senate
numerously signed by citizens of Philadelphia. He said that he could not advocate
the prayer it contained, nor consent to the
requirement of twenty-one years' residence.
He was opposed to any change in the natu-

[1] (438) *House Journal,* Twenty-eighth Congress, First Session,
433.

[2] *Ibid.,* 357; February 7, 1844.　　　[3] *Ibid.,* 706, 717.

ralization laws. The memorialists, however, were anxious for a decision as early as possible, and he thought that there were imperative reasons why it should be made. He moved reference to the Judiciary Committee, and expressed his strong desire that they report with as little delay as possible. Twice thereafter he repeated his strong desire for a speedy report.[4]

Sturgeon presented one of the petitions, and was far from concurring in the necessity for the action sought. It was his conviction that foreigners ought to be entitled to citizenship as soon as they were ready to give satisfactory proof of a preference for the country and its institutions such as induced them to make it a permanent residence. Since it was difficult to act on a presumption of intentions, he believed that the law as it stood was, on the whole, best calculated to obviate all difficulties. He thought that foreigners ought not to object to the restriction, since in many states native citizens could not enjoy the privileges of state citizenship till after two years' residence.[5] There was further discussion a few days later [6] upon the

[4] *Congressional Globe,* Twenty-eighth Congress, First Session, 675; June 1, 1844.

[5] *Ibid.*, 691, June 6, 1844.

[6] June 11, 1844.

presentation of two memorials from Philadelphia asking for twenty-one years' residence and "more solemn sanctions." Archer
said that the time was too short before adjournment to admit of the possibility of decided action.   On a proper occasion, if no
other person did so, he would make the
necessary motion to secure the object of the petitioners. Berrien, of the Judiciary Committee, said that this was a question of the greatest importance and had been so considered
from the foundation of the government. Recently it had been productive of great excitement, the result of which was deeply to be
deplored.[7] This prayer was presented at a
very late period of the session, when the committee had a variety of matter before it. He believed it was too late to secure deliberate action
of the committee.

Allen was utterly opposed to any such

[7] The diary of John Quincy Adams, for May 9, 1844, explained what he termed a new subject of political excitement that
must have great influence for good or evil "(God grant it may be
for good)" upon the future history and fortunes of the Union.
There was a deadly feud between the native American poor population and the Roman Catholic Irish multitudes gathered in the city
of Philadelphia.   Animosities between those classes had been fer-
menting in all the Atlantic cities for several years, much aggravated by the pernicious factious influence of Irish Catholics over
the elections in all the populous cities.   The reaction of the native
American population had effected a total revolution at the recent
election of the city government of New York, and had just broken
out in furious riots in Philadelphia, where from the first of the
week a succession of bitterly exasperated mobs had destroyed multitudes of human lives, dwelling-houses, schools, and churches, unrestrained by the government of the city or of the state   (XII, 24).

change of laws to the prejudice of the people. It involved manifest injustice and inhumanity. Nothing could tend more to exasperate the feelings of men, disturb harmony, and excite hostility to their institutions in the very bosom of the country. He should resist it to the utmost.[8] Benton presented two memorials, but was opposed to their prayer, agreed with Allen, and was favorable to the largest liberty.[9]

On June 15, 1844, Berrien reported for the Senate Committee on Judiciary on sundry memorials before it. The question was one of awakening interest and affected a policy little varied from the commencement of the government. The memorialists thought that changes in conditions rendered proper a modification of the laws. The committee was disposed to treat their suggestions with deserved respect, and to give the questions involved the most deliberate consideration. But it was obviously impracticable to give them the needed consideration, and impossible that any action should be had, at that session. They therefore asked to be discharged from further consideration of the subject.[10]

[8] Congressional Globe, Twenty-eighth Congress, First Session, 658; June 11, 1844.

[9] Ibid., 658, 686.

[10] (436) Senate Documents, Twenty-eighth Congress, First Session, 395.

In the House during this session three different members gave notice of a motion to be made for leave to introduce a bill to amend the naturalization laws, but it does not appear that any bills were introduced upon the subject.   John Quincy Adams presented a Pennsylvania petition praying for such amendments to the naturalization laws that twenty-one years' residence after they had declared their intentions should be made the indispensable prerequisite to the admission of foreigners into the inestimable rights of American citizens.   Adams said that he presented the petition in a formal way because it related to a subject of considerable importance upon which there was considerable difference of opinion.   He was willing to afford the unknown petitioners the satisfaction of having their matter brought pointedly before the House; but he would not bind himself in any way to support their prayer.   In his diary he wrote that he presented the petition of 180 Native Americans of Philadelphia praying for a change in the naturalization laws and twenty-five years' [11] residence for political rights; but he did not approve of the change in the law, and felt obliged to

[11] Either "twenty-five" was used as a round number, and may thus indicate the newness of the twenty-one year agitation, or it is an evident error.   The *House Journal* is explicit with reference to this petition.

say that he could not support it. He had
moved its reference to the Committee on Judiciary, but a motion to lay on the table, by
Brown (Ind.) and Hammett (Miss.), had
carried by a vote of 128 to 26.[12]

After two weeks Adams secured the removal of the petition from the table and its
reference to the Judiciary Committee. Near
the close of the session he was seeking a copy
of it of the clerk, and intending to see whether
the National Intelligencer would publish it.
He wrote that it was the first memorial on
the subject presented to the House, and
predicted that at the next session of Congress
the Native American party would be heard
in both houses, when the proceedings of the
House on that first memorial would have a
material influence on the debate.[13]

The extreme note in the Native American
agitation of this period was perhaps struck
in a work on the Civil Government of the
Hebrews by Professor Wines. He would
welcome the immigrants fleeing from wrongs,
but go to Moses for a public policy and study
the principle of his naturalization laws. Admission to citizenship was called "entering
into the congregation of Jehovah." Certain

[12] *Memoirs*, XII, 40.

[13] (438) *House Journal,* Twenty-eighth Congress, First Session,
988, 1130; *Congressional Globe,* Twenty-eighth Congress, First
Session, 633; May 31, 1844; J. Q. Adams' *Memoirs*, XII, 40, 65.

races were not to be admitted to the tenth generation—in other words, never. Some other foreigners could become Israelitish citizens in the third generation. In other words, the grandchildren of immigrants could be admitted to the privileges of natives of the soil. Thus naturalization in sentiments, habits, sympathies, and manners was required before privileges were given by a legal naturalization. The principle must commend itself, but need not always be applied in equal rigor.[14]

During the next session of Congress thirty Native American petitions found mention in the *Senate Journal,* and a larger number were received by the House, including some of the former ones. A resolution by Johnson instructed the Senate Judiciary Committee to inquire into the expediency of modifying the laws to extend the term allowed to enable foreigners to become citizens, to require greater guards against fraud in the steps to be taken in procuring naturalization papers, and to prevent, as far as practicable, fraud and violence at elections. To this resolution was added by an amendment, "and prohibit the introduction of foreign convicts into the United States." [15]

[14] *Niles Register,* LXVII, 162.

[15] (448) *Senate Journal,* Twenty-eighth Congress, Second Session, 30.

A resolution submitted by Barrow a little later gave similar instructions for an inquiry to be made whether naturalization papers had been granted to foreigners by any federal or state court in violation of the provisions of the laws of Congress; also with regard to empowering the district court to cancel and declare null all naturalization papers which were found, upon judicial investigation, to have been granted in violation or fraud of the laws of Congress.[16]

The Johnson resolution called forth some vigorous expressions of opinion before it was referred. Johnson held that the facilities with which foreigners had been naturalized for a few years past, the perjuries committed, the fraud and violence controlling elections, proved the necessity of an immediate change in the naturalization laws. There was no doubt that public sentiment everywhere called loudly for prompt action. Thousands of foreigners were naturalized and voted within a few weeks after reaching America. In New York City alone over three thousand persons were naturalized a few days before an election. A Philadelphia vigilance committee had reported 305 votes in a single ward, and not one of the persons was found after ten

[16] *Loc. cit.*, 40, 44.

days. The laws had been valuable at first,
and had brought much development and
many good citizens. Now the country was
strong and did not need outside strength.
There was no longer need to invite knowledge by promising political privileges.[17]
Some desirable persons might continue to
come, but the mass was not desirable. He
would grant property rights, but require a
long residence for political rights. They
must prohibit the sending of convicts and
paupers. The question was one far above
party considerations, and all were equally in-
terested in guarding against dangers.

Archer said that there was very great
solicitude in the question by the people. He
believed in his very conscience that it had
become the most important question that
could agitate the public mind. It was more
than transcendental in magnitude and importance, comprehending every other vital issue.
He hoped for an early report.

Rives had no hesitation in favoring an inquiry as to frauds. There was no doubt as to
the alarming extent of the abuses. He would
not exclude nor unreasonably restrain naturalization; and would give every foreigner,

[17] This was a reference to an idea, not met with often, nor
for a long time before, namely, that liberal naturalization laws were
necessary to attract skilled and educated foreigners who would
be particularly serviceable to the country.

when naturalized, his fair and just share in the government. The long and successful policy of the past seemed to him wise and prudent. But the practice had degenerated into a public mockery, and idle, empty form. A ridiculous pantomime made full-blown citizens, by platoons of twenty to fifty at the clerk's desk, of persons ignorant of the language. It was so in New York. Buffalo, Philadelphia, and probably in Louisiana. The evil came from relaxations from original provisions of the law. The remedy was to reinvigorate the present laws. Registry of arrival was important, and a full record in the certificate of naturalization. Making the declaration to a clerk, and the reduction of the time required for it from three to two years, were among the sources of the evils; also the repeal in 1828 of Jefferson's and Madison's provisions. It would be time enough to extend the period after restoring and trying those provisions.

Merrick thought that the excitement should be directed against their own people who had abused the laws. Dickinson said that the resolutions apparently were not aimed at abuses, but at the system. It was impossible to improve men's condition by denying them political rights and privileges.

Foster thought that persons unfit for citizenship in five years after their arrival would be after twenty years. There was no moral test applied to those who were born in the United States. Berrien said that it was scarcely practicable to have a very prompt report. Great frauds were alleged, and considerable frauds seemed to be almost universally admitted. Judging from the magnitude and delicacy of the inquiry, a prompt report was not to be expected.[18]

Buchanan, in remarks at the presentation of a memorial the next day, was against extending the five-year period. If frauds as charged were established, he would go with the farthest-going in amending the laws to prevent them.

Archer was extremely anxious ᴎ express his sentiments, but that was not the time for them. He perceived that there was to be a hot war in the country in relation to the subject, and was deeply concerned at the indications of the previous day's debate. He had hoped before that an impression had been produced on the Senate such as he knew prevailed in the country. He was grieved not to see that feeling there, but was glad that the people knew the Senate's position

[18] *Congressional Globe*, 32; December, 16, 1844.

so early. It was not enough to cut off excrescences; they must eradicate the root of the evil. If the Senate did not give redress, the people would.

A request from the Senate, made at the instance of Berrien of the Judiciary Committee,[19] brought a report from the secretary of state as to the practice of foreign governments in transporting paupers and criminals to the United States. Aside from a letter from Hamburg in 1832, showing that a number of persons from prisons and houses of correction, claimed mostly to be guilty of boyish indiscretions, had been released and given passports to North America, nothing of consequence was shown in addition to what was in the report made in 1838.[20]

Five weeks before the expiration of the Twenty-Eighth Congress, Berrien made a preliminary report for the Senate Judiciary Committee. They had given earnest attention to the subject, on account both of its intrinsic importance and of the public feeling manifested in regard to it. They had issued commissions that were in process of execution, and had "prepared a bill meanwhile cal-

[19] (448) *Senate Journal,* Twenty-eighth Congress, Second Session, 50.

[20] (450) *Senate Documents,* Twenty-eighth Congress, Second Session, No. 42.

culated to supply the more prominent defects" of the existing system. They submitted it on account of the short time remaining and the importance of action at that session, postponing further report until returns
should be received from the commissions.[21]

A second report from Berrien's committee
was made March 3, 1845, just at the close
of the Twenty-Eighth Congress.[22] The commissions for taking testimony in New York,
Philadelphia, and Baltimore had completed
their work too late for the committee to do
more than present abstracts from the testimony they had taken. The New Orleans
commission reported later.

The investigation in New York was
thorough, and included the collection of much
testimony from judges, and clerks of courts,
political workers, and others. A great deal
of light is thrown upon the practical work-
ings of the naturalization law in several
classes of courts. Judge Hammond, of the
Marine Court for the Southern District of
New York, testified that for the first six of
his ten years' service as a judge his court had
probably naturalized more persons than any
other one court of New York. Declarations

[21] *Ibid.*, No. 59.
[22] (458) *ibid.*, No. 173; March 3, 1845.

and depositions were printed in blank and bound up in books for record. They were signed by the party and sworn to. A certificate was taken away. Only one witness was required, except for those showing residence between 1802 and 1812. He always examined persons orally; they subscribed their names and were sworn on the Bible. The character of the applicant, and his attitude toward the government and the Constitution, were sworn to by the witness. He was not cross-examined with regard to them. Others testified to the same procedure in this respect in other courts, and that it was very much a matter of form or entirely nugatory, as questions were seldom asked. A witness was never known to hesitate to swear to these particulars.

Since about 1839 or 1840 the Marine Court had interpreted literally the requirement of five years' residence in the United States. It had excluded eight persons in one week for having been out of the United States during their residence period. Before the time mentioned this requirement had been generally overlooked. Decisions upon this point in other courts had conflicted. A duplicate certificate of naturalization was given when the original had been lost or destroyed.

The facts were sworn to if there was doubt
about them.   The judge knew of one case of
a witness being convicted who had made a
practice of testifying for applicants.   Naturalization was the only business the law allowed to be done on election day.   About
eighty in an eight-hour day was the most
they had naturalized.   At other than election
times they averaged perhaps three or four
a week.   The clerk had once counted up
eighteen hundred naturalizations in a year.
Two thousand would probably be the extreme number, and some years the number
was probably not one thousand.   The clerk
attended to the fees.   A former clerk had
probably compounded the fees, making an
arrangement by which voucher slips were
presented drawing on a sum of money deposited with him.

Another justice of the Marine Court had
known the same person to get several duplicate certificates of his declaration of intention.   It was easy to get a duplicate after a
naturalization in another court.   The examination was always oral, and often fifteen or
twenty a day were rejected.   Naturalizations
at election times were mostly due to the inducement of others.   At other times of the
year they were usually for the purpose of

holding real estate. He had observed one political witness who appeared to be employed for the purpose of giving testimony. Papers filled out in writing and in print had come to his court addressed to other courts. The parties bringing them had said that they got them at Tammany Hall and were sent there. An interpreter was often required— at the time of the last election in the case of nearly half of the applicants. Arrangements with committees had been made frequently by the former clerk, and tickets drawing upon a sum of money deposited had been accepted in place of fees. Papers had been withheld until the parties had voted.

Another justice said that perjuries had been complained of to him. The courts' refusal to arrange with committees had driven the principal business to other courts. One judge could naturalize from fifty to a hundred persons in seven hours. The number would depend upon the intelligence of the parties, etc., and upon the care taken.

Judge Vanderpoel, of the New York Superior Court, knew of no fraud. Before the decision of the State Supreme Court in October, 1844, persons domiciled in the United States for five years, and sailors on the packets with families in the United States, had been naturalized. The chief justice had told him that a decision favored this practice. When applicants were numerous, they were sworn by the clerk either in open court or in the clerk's office. They came next to this judge, who administered the general oath to the witness and indorsed the papers when he had approved them. In cases of doubt he examined them critically. The applicant and his witness then went into open court before another judge who was holding court, and took the printed oaths. In a majority of cases the applicants came with their preliminary papers filled out. He believed that this was done by a naturalization committee in session at Tammany Hall, or by their opponents.

Henry Raymond testified that he arranged for the use of tickets recently, as he had done for years. There might have been a thousand or fifteen hundred tickets.[23] The parties paid their own fees if they were able. His committee employed a dozen clerks who prepared papers and filled up affidavits.

Henry E. Riell testified that he was president of the Naturalization Society of New

[23] Other testimony showed that a printed ticket was used with the names written in, in form as follows:

"NEW YORK, Apr. 17, 1840.

"The Marine Court will please naturalize George Terry.
Endorsed: "Burlington, N. J."   JAMES JOHN VALENTINE."

York City. Its members were generally Democrats.. He made out most of the papers for Tammany. It was customary to advertise that the committee was in session. Tickets were issued, and he redeemed them. They were generally given to poor people—those who wished to pay their own fees went directly to the court. The usual number naturalized through the agency of the committee at spring and fall elections was about one thousand, except that in the fall of 1840 about three thousand were naturalized in five months. The parties invariably received their certificates at the time of their admission, and voted for whom they pleased.[24] They came to his committee voluntarily in all cases, and he took it for granted that they were Democrats.

Other evidence indicated that the Whig committees had for a time pursued similar methods, but for two years past had resolved not to do so longer.

The report of the Philadelphia commission dealt mainly with the numbers naturalized in various courts, and the fees charged. It showed, however, that sixty-four declarations of intention, fraudulently interpolated in the records of a court, and dated back two years

---

[24] Other testimony was to the effect that certificates were sometimes withheld until after the parties had voted.

to admit of the prompt naturalization of the
parties, had been discovered and annulled a
few days before the election of 1840.   At
Baltimore various cases of fraudulent voting
by using dead men's naturalization papers
were discovered.   The New Orleans report
dealt with the testimony in the impeachment
of a judge who was removed in 1844 for
naturalizing with great haste, carelessness,
informality, and disregard of legal requirements.   The reports show that the number
of persons naturalized varied greatly in the
different courts.   It was much greater in the
state courts, where the fees were lower and
the requirements generally less rigid.   Naturalizations were largely had within two
weeks of election days.

The fees varied greatly, being much higher
in federal than in state courts.   They were
often reduced by arrangement with political
committees.   The legal fees ranged from 50
cents to $3 for naturalization, and from 20
cents to $1.25 for a declaration of intention.
The fees had recently been much reduced in
the New York state courts.

There were many recommendations made
by the witnesses, most of which were for the
purpose of preventing fraud or of securing
better-qualified citizens.   The more   important

ant of them were already embodied in the bill
of the committee before the commissions had
finished their work. There was little demand
for a long term of residence, but a general
desire that a residence for six months or a
year after naturalization should precede suffrage. One would shorten the five-year term
by this period. Others would prohibit naturalization for some time before an election. Many
would confine naturalization to United States
courts, and there was a suggestion that
special United States courts be established
for naturalizing. A previous notice of intention shortly before the application was
favored. This should be served on the district attorney or a federal officer; or a notice
with names of witnesses should be published.
A certificate of declaration of intention should
be evidence of the time of arrival in the
United States. Again, applicants should be
required to swear to their term of residence.
They should also swear to their attachment
to the Constitution, and to being well disposed to the government. A description of
the person should be in the declaration of intention and in the certificate of naturalization, so that one person could not use the
papers of another. The papers should be
indorsed with signature, if the person could

write, and the certificate should be produced
at the polls. Vessels should deposit a list
and description of all persons brought to the
United States. Candidates for naturalization
should understand and speak the English
language, and should expressly abjure all
temporal allegiance to the pope. Congress
should fix all fees and forbid remitting any
part of them; or again there should be no
fees allowed. Persons should be punished
for applying for naturalization in another
court after having been once rejected. A
wide door for fraud was in the granting of
duplicate certificates of declaration of intention. Sometimes fifty a day of these were applied for in a single court at election time.

Meanwhile the bill before the senate was
entirely ignored to the end of the Congress.
Its leading features were compulsory record
of arrivals to form documentary evidence of
length of residence, naturalization restricted
to United States courts and to times remote
from elections, the process of naturalization
more minutely specified, fraud of any sort to
be punished severely, and the naturalization
secured by it to be annulled. The bill provided that collectors of customs should receive
reports of aliens arriving in the United
States, and register in a book of record full

descriptions of their persons, with countries, times and places of arrival, and vessels, places of residence in the United States, and members of their families. The declaration of intention to become a citizen could be made only in United States circuit and district courts, at least three years after the registry of arrival, upon petition and production of a duly authenticated certificate of registry. It must contain a full description as before, be subscribed in a book of record together with oath as to being the person described in the certificate, be sworn to in the presence of the judge of the court, and attested by him. Two years later the alien could be naturalized in a similar court upon presenting a petition setting forth the circumstances of his case. His certificate of registry and declaration must be given up, canceled, and filed. The court must be satisfied, after examination, of his identity, of the genuineness of his certificates, lack of fraud, residence (five years and one year, as before), character, and disposition (as before), and that he had not been convicted of any felony. These facts were to be proved by citizens of the United States, whose names, residence, and occupations must appear in the record and in the certificate. Support of the Constitution must be promised, and the usual renunciation of foreign allegiance made. When the court was satisfied, it might decree admission to citizenship, and direct a certificate to be granted under seal of the court, signed by judge and clerk. The certificate must contain a copy of the registry with full description and particulars, and both the record and the certificates must show that all requirements of the law had been met. No admission could take place except by express order of the court declared in the records.

Any person who had been registered while under sixteen as a part of the family of an alien, and had continued his residence the required time, might be naturalized according to law without producing a certificate of registry or a previous declaration of intention.

No second certificate could be granted without proof of loss of the first by accident, and two months' public advertising for it, and then only to the party, or to his legal representative if dead.

Proper certificates of two years' war-time service by an able-bodied male person at least seventeen years of age at enlistment should be evidence authorizing naturalization on taking the oath of allegiance and making the required renunciations. No decree of naturalization could be made within —— months of any general election in the state or district, and no rights were conferred outside of the state or district for —— months after naturalization. No alien enemy could be naturalized. No proof should be admitted or received of any facts made a matter of record, except the certificate of the record. Any attempted fraud by any person in naturalization was made a high misdemeanor. The court having decreed a naturalization could re-examine the same at any time within five years, upon petition of any citizens, or upon its own motion; and if fraud, wilful irregularity, or gross negligence appeared, it must rescind and reverse the decree, and declare the naturalization to be utterly null and void. Any alien already in the United States who should at any time within six months prove five years' residence within the United States, and that he was in all other respects, except as to a certificate of registry, entitled to naturalization under the new act, could be admitted to citizenship by a decree of the court. All conflicting provisions of former laws were repealed.[25]

In the House a motion was "laid over" that sought the institution of an inquiry as to the

[25] (458) *Senate Documents,* Twenty-eighth Congress, Second Session, No. 173, 198.

expediency of a law to authorize taking the testimony of absent witnesses. The plan suggested was for the court, upon the motion of an applicant, to issue a commission authorizing any justice of the peace or clerk of a court where the witnesses resided to take their testimony in writing, certify to it, and send it to be used as competent evidence to secure the applicant the benefit of the naturalization law. While this plan would doubtless have been very serviceable to many honest applicants, the abundant enlargement of the opportunity for fraud that it would have made must have prevented its acceptance, even at a time when the necessity for guarding the franchise was less prominently in the public mind, and when political wisdom could be found in legislating in the interest of aliens.[26]

A motion for a similar inquiry as to a law to require that the name of every emigrant should be registered at the custom-house, and a certificate of such registration be the indispensable proof of the term of his residence in the United States; also as to a law that the right of suffrage should not be granted until two years after naturalization; and as to any other amendments necessary

[26] (462) *House Journal,* Twenty-eighth Congress, Second Session, 96; December 17, 1844.

for the pervention of frauds and the preservation of the purity of the elective franchise, was laid over under the rules, on notice of debate.[27] Its proposal that Congress should legislate to control the right of suffrage is rather remarkable for this period.

The House Judiciary Committee reported[28] on the petitions referred to it, and presented a bill to establish a uniform rule of naturalization, and to repeal all other acts or parts of acts on that subject. The report first analyzed all former acts, both existing and obsolete. It said that the laws were liberal, simple, and easily understood, and had undergone no change for seventeen years. They might require condensation for convenience and perspicuity, and some amendments to prevent imposition and fraud. But the petitioners asked for a radical change in the residence requirement, which the committee supposed, in the words of Jefferson, "would in effect operate as a denial of the privilege altogether." Such a restriction would conflict with the policy of each and all the states in their early settlement, and control the former liberal policy of the federal government. The right to emigrate, and the privilege of

[27] *Congressional Globe,* Twenty-eighth Congress, Second Session, 64; December 23, 1844.

[28] January 31, 1845.

being naturalized under provisions the least
onerous and restrictive, were everywhere
recognized in state laws and constitutions.
The principle involved, the right to renounce
an allegiance by birth and not by choice, was
acknowledged from the constitution of New
Hampshire to that of Louisiana. The Declaration of Independence had complained of
England that she "obstructed the laws of
naturalization of foreigners." The constitutional clause for naturalization met with not
the slightest objection either in forming or
adopting the Constitution. The secretary of
state reported of foreign governments that
they all used aliens in war against their native country, even when not regularly naturalized, and that they allowed their own subjects to emigrate.

But why multiply references and examples in support
of the principle and right of emigration and expatriation,
in contradistinction to the doctrine of native allegiance, and
the disavowal of naturalization — a doctrine which belongs
to those dark and gloomy periods when conquest fettered
the persons, and superstition weighed down the minds of
men.

Greece, Rome, and modern France were
better models. The French constitution of
1791 had made the single condition of naturalization: "those who—being born out of the
kingdom,   of   foreign   parents—reside   in

France, become French citizens after five years' continued residence in the kingdom." The seven- and nine-year periods for office for foreigners, in the Constitution, were not in harmony with this twenty-one-year period, by which thirty years were required after the declaration of intention. The petitioners seemed to suppose that increase of population was the only object of naturalization laws. It was one object, but not the only one. The committee would say: "It was to assert the great principle of expatriation, and the right of every man to leave the country of his birth for the one of his choice." Not merely the new states, but many of the old ones also, would gladly add to their strength and wealth by an increase of their numbers. If frauds were practiced, guard against them by amendments. Were they practiced only or chiefly by the naturalized, or also by natives? The committee thought it advisable to collect all naturalization provisions into one general law, and believed that the bill it presented, if adopted, would carry out the injunctions of the Constitution, preserve the rights of aliens, and guard against all just grounds of abuse and complaint.[29]

The bill that the committee presented con-

[29] (468) *House Reports of Committees,* Twenty-eighth Congress, Second Session, No. 87.

tained ten sections. It was chiefly a re-enact-
ment of the existing law, with some additional provisions to remedy minor defects, to
make fraudulent practices more difficult, and
to secure the punishment of fraud. Any alien
free white was to be admitted a citizen of
the United States in the mode and on the
conditions given, and not otherwise. He
must declare on oath in open court before a
supreme, superior, district, or circuit court of
a state or territory, or a circuit or district
court of the United States, at least two years
before his admission, his intention to become
a citizen, and to renounce his foreign allegiance. Two years later, and after five years'
residence in the United States, he might be
admitted a citizen, provided he took an oath
that he would support the Constitution and
did renounce any other allegiance and any
title; exhibited a certificate of his declaration
of intention, and took an oath that he was
the person named therein; furnished two witnesses, citizens, who should swear that they
were well acquainted with him and believed
him to be the person named in the certificate,
and that he had resided five years in the
United States and one year in that state; and
proved that he was of good moral character,
attached to the principles of the Constitu-

tion, and well disposed to the good order and happiness of the country. The full particulars of his certificate, residence, names of witnesses, etc., must be stated in the record. Otherwise it should not be competent for any court to grant a certificate of naturalization or pronounce a judgment of naturalization, nor should the person be deemed a citizen of the United States.

Any minor living in the United States for two years before he was twenty-one, and thereafter, might, after becoming twenty-one and after five years of residence, be admitted without the previous declaration of intention, provided that he made the declaration at the time of his admission, and declared and proved that it had been for three years his *bona fide* intention to become a citizen, and complied with all the other requirements. When any alien died after having declared his intention, his widow and children, dwelling in the United States, should be considered citizens upon taking the oath and renouncing their former allegiance. Minor children of naturalized citizens dwelling in the United States should be considered citizens. The children of free white citizens, born out of the United States during a temporary absence of their parents, should be deemed native citizens.

Every court of record of any state, having common law jurisdiction and a seal and clerk, should be considered a district court within the meaning of the act. Any declaration before the passage of the act made *bona fide* before the clerk of an authorized court should be held as valid as if made before the court. Clerks of courts should grant certificates of declaration, and receive a fee of one dollar each for granting and recording them; also a fee of two dollars for a naturalization certificate to be paid before the naturalization was allowed. Fraudulent application or naturalization was to be a high misdemeanor, and be punished by a fine of not more than one thousand dollars, or by imprisonment of not more than six months, or by both. Anyone knowingly aiding in the fraud was liable to one-half of the specified penalties. A fraudulent naturalization was to be void. It should be the duty of a district attorney learning of fraud to file an information; *scire facias* should then issue to show why the naturalization should not be null; and if it was shown by confession, default, or jury trial that the naturalization had been procured by fraud, it was to be the duty of the court to adjudge it to be null and void. Knowingly and wilfully using or permitting the use of any certificate of declaration or of naturalization, except for the proper person and lawfully, should be a misdemeanor, liable to one-half of the before-mentioned penalties. All other acts and parts of acts respecting naturalization were to be repealed.[30] This bill was referred, after two readings, to the Committee of the Whole House on the State of the Union, and had not come up for consideration when the session and the Congress ended a month later.

[30] *Congressional Globe,* Twenty-eighth Congress, Second Session, Appendix, 130; January 31, 1845.

CHAPTER XIII

THE PERIOD OF AGGRESSIVE NATIVE AMERI-
CANISM (CONTINUED)

In July, 1845, a Native American national
convention was held at Philadelphia, with
delegates present from nine states. It set
forth its principles in a number of resolutions, formally took the name "Native Americans," and sent out an address called "The
Second Declaration of Independence." The
resolutions declared that they could give
their suffrages only to persons *born on the
soil,* and favored twenty-one years' residence
for foreigners thereafter naturalized. They
would kindly receive persons who came to
America, and give them every privilege except office and suffrage.

Archer, during the next session of the
Senate, presented thirty memorials for
"twenty-one years" legislation. Three-
fourths of them were from Pennsylvania.
They were referred, and no other action was
taken on the subject.

In the House the naturalization question
attained much greater prominence. A series
of resolutions of the Massachusetts Legis-

lature was presented early in the session, and the question of its reference brought on a prolonged debate.[31]   According to the resolutions, experience had clearly shown that the naturalization laws were loose and defective, affording opportunity for gross frauds, destructive to the rights and morals of the citizens and the stability of their institutions. The rights, interests, and morals of the people demanded an immediate and thorough revision of the naturalization laws. The legislature regarded it as the imperative duty of Congress so to amend those laws. While a liberal and just policy should be adopted toward foreigners who were in the country or might come there, the rights and privileges of their own countrymen should be kept inviolate and the ballot box be permanently guarded against improper influence. The solid Whig delegation of nine members that Massachusetts had in the House, and her senators, were especially requested to use their utmost exertions forthwith to procure amendments in accord with the views expressed.[32]

Levin, for some time thereafter a striking Native American figure in House or Senate, ob-

[31] This debate began December 15, and was continued on December 17, 18, 29, and 30.

[32] *House Journal,* Twenty-ninth Congress, First Session, 96.

jected to referring the bill to the Judiciary Committee on the ground of established usage or privilege of the House, which (he said) secured to a measure full and fair discussion on its merits from a committee that was not prejudiced against its main principle. The doctrine was clearly laid down that those opposed to the main principle of a bill were not to be appointed its judges. Reference to a committee known to be hostile was tantamount to a rejection, and that was prejudgment that would suit a sultan. The eyes of the nation were turned on the House. The people loved this child of theirs, "monster" as it had been called. They expected consideration for it, and Congress could not grant a smaller act of justice. Giddings inquired whether Levin had not always voted at that session to smother petitions against slavery of eighty thousand native-born Americans. Brodhead questioned where there was evidence of any disposition on the part of the Judiciary Committee to smother the matter. There was none on which to found so offensive an imputation. Why let the American party select a committee? Must the House dignify by a report of a select committee what but six out of two hundred and twenty-three representatives of the whole American people professed to advocate? So very small a minority must be treated as other minorities were treated. How was it to be expected that the majority would endorse the opposing view? He called for the previous question to save time from useless discussion, but withdrew it at the request of Rathbun, chairman of the Judiciary Committee.

Rathbun favored granting the request of Levin. If the memorial was sent to his committee, he should move to discharge it at the first meeting. Let the few there have the nursing of this new and original thought of theirs as to naturalization, and present the bantling when sufficiently grown. Let them show that the previous course of the nation was all wrong, and that a foreigner should not vote until the infant born on the day of his arrival voted at his side. Maclay regretted Rathbun's willingness. Two years before he would have granted willingly the reference asked, on account of the prominence in the public discussions that the subject seemed to occupy. There was a great change since, and the public judgment had been pronounced. The miserable Native American movement no longer excited the regard of an intelligent community. It never had any strength except in large cities, and could not

stand country atmosphere.[33]   Let the Judiciary Committee examine the subject patient-
ly, and report showing the sheer absurdity óf
any change in the system that had prevailed
from the foundation of the government and
was the cause of so large a part of the country's prosperity.   McDowell was utterly opposed to twenty-one years, but had no objection to revision for the more effectual protection of the ballot box.   But if the object
was to get up political excitement in the
House, and send out nourishment to a party
fast dwindling into insignificance, he would
vote to table the memorial.   Payne (Ala.) believed the present movement was one to get
up a faction in the House such as the Anti-
Mason and Abolition factions, and hoped for
a merited rebuke for it.   Yancey (Ala.) believed it ever the practice to refer a matter
to its friends, and favored a special committee to meet the matter fairly.

Others thought that, though the Native
Americans were few and feeble, yet they were
entitled to courtesy and a fair hearing.
There was not a native American on the Ju-

[33] Later, another speaker, either John W. Davis (Ind.) or
Jefferson Davis, declared that the Native American party was generated by the corruption of the great cities, and could not live
in the pure atmosphere of the country—that nobody had ever
heard of a meeting of Native Americans in a country schoolhouse.
Native Americans were but a wing of the Whigs.   Open doors
to immigration was the true policy of the government.

diciary Committee, and there could not be even a minority report from it. What harm could a select committee do—there had been a bill and a report at the last session, but no action? These measures marked the incipient stage of making a great alien class. The Native American party had its birth in a storm—one of the most wretched and disgraceful scenes ever seen in Philadelphia— and was everywhere declared to be seeking the offices that were held by the foreign-born. The question was entitled to no more respect than Abolition.[34] The attempt to divert the reference was an acknowledgment that they were seeking to throw firebrands, and to send out an inflammatory report to make converts for Native Americanism.

Levin replied that so strong and attractive a principle as that of the Native Americans yet promised a majority of the House and the country. In fifteen years the native-born would be in a minority. Americans were shot down in Philadelphia on the plea that they were on the Irish quarter, and that no Americans were allowed there. They were charged falsely with being "burners of churches." They had saved a church at the risk of their lives, and had destroyed none. They were neither bigots nor fanatics.

[34] This was from Chipman, a Democrat from Michigan.

Bayly (Va.) regarded the resolutions as a bold attempt to interfere with the acknowledged rights of states. The general government had no jurisdiction in the matter and could not control suffrage. They could do no more than to deprive the foreigner of his right to the habeas corpus, to hold property, and other rights pertaining to citizenship. His right to suffrage was exclusively under the jurisdiction of the states. The measure proposed would deter men of property and character from coming, but would hardly keep out paupers. He could not consent to take a great constitutional question from the law committee and refer it to a special committee.

Bayly's constitutional argument ignored the important fact that the states had, very generally and largely as a matter of course, made United States citizenship a qualification for suffrage, and that perhaps in most of them a change of opinion as to their legal right would be necessary before that requirement could be removed. It followed that a federal law hindering naturalization would act effectively to deprive the majority of foreigners of their rights to the suffrage. To be sure, some states were then asserting, and perhaps all would today acknowledge, their legal power to overcome this difficulty; but most states then thought it to be either illegal or unwise to take such action. So long and so far as this opinion prevailed, Congress had actual control of the situation. A remarkable fact to notice, also, is that Bayly did not claim for the states any control over the right to hold property. I think that the explanation of this must be found in the federal ownership and control of the sale of the public lands, and the importance assumed by the public lands among the possible property holdings of aliens. In other words, the property right then meant to an alien the right to buy public lands.

Stephen A. Douglas said that naturalization conferred the right of citizenship, which included the rights of protection, access to the courts in time of war, holding real estate, inheritance, and various other rights. The federal convention had discussed the matter of fixing uniform rules of voting, and abandoned it. The differences were too many and too great to reconcile or remove, and it became necessary to split or compromise. The right of each state to qualify voters had never been questioned.[35] The states defied and

[35] A very inadequate statement. An absolute right, not subject to the limitations of the naturalization laws, had been denied often in Congress and elsewhere.

derided the attempts of the Native Americans to control the suffrage by naturalization. The Judiciary Committee of the last Congress had offered a bill to remedy frauds. Also there was now a different committee. If there had been any fault before, it was that of Congress rather than of the committee.

In closing the debate, two members defended the Whig party from responsibility for Native Americanism. It had arisen in Democratic districts in the outskirts of Philadelphia. Democratic loss of the Irish vote had started it. The party was of no practical use to anybody but Democrats. Whig Ohio had denounced it in resolutions of the legislature. That it had sprung from the Democratic party as its source could be demonstrated. The debate was ended only with the previous question. The resolutions were sent to the Judiciary Committee December 30, 1845.[36]

The committee presented an emphatic report on the 10th of February. They had waited some weeks for proofs of the statements in the resolutions, but none had been offered them. The time of the resolutions had been least favorable for an unprejudiced examination of the truth of the matters, owing

[36] *Congressional Globe*, Twenty-ninth Congress, First Session, 67-74, 77-82, 105-7, 113-18.

to the great excitement in the election of 1844. Complaint had naturally followed defeat. It was difficult to perceive dangers from the naturalization laws or from the votes of naturalized persons. The committee understood the resolutions to complain only of looseness of the laws and opportunity for fraud upon them. The judge and the clerk were in this, the same as in their other duties, under a legal and moral responsibility to administer the laws honestly and justly. A violation of this duty was a high crime. Witnesses were all liable for perjury. The committee was unable to devise any greater penalties for perjury in harmony with the humane spirit of the age. It would be regarded as barbarous and inhumane to forfeit life. They were constrained to believe that the naturalization laws were sufficiently guarded and sufficiently stringent. Some thought that the period of probation should be twenty-one years. The committee thought differently and were sustained by experience. The longer the probation, the greater was the inducement to fraud. It was impolitic to perpetuate the character of alien longer than was absolutely necessary. If all foreigners who had come for twenty years were still aliens, and excluded from all rights in soil and government, consider the danger, especially in case of war with England. Her subjects, embittered and denied rights, could not aid the United States. Nor could or would the United States protect aliens. It was wise and prudent to Americanize the whole class as speedily as possible. The reasons for liberal naturalization laws still existed in all their force. They ought not to be disregarded, nor ought any disadvantageous or repulsive restrictions to be added to the laws. When the population became dense, labor cheap, employment scarce, then, and not till then, would it be necessary to inquire as to a change. The states controlled suffrage, and had the remedy for evils in themselves. They could, but ought not to, proscribe naturalized citizens. The committee had no knowledge of frauds nor evidence concerning them. They would not look among ignorant aliens for perpetrators of frauds. These might be instruments in the hands of unprincipled citizens. They recommended a resolution: that no alteration of the naturalization laws is necessary for the preservation of rights, interests, and morals of the people, or for the guarding of the ballot box from every improper influence.[37]

[37] (489) *House Reports of Committees*, Twenty-ninth Congress, First Session, No. 231.

Two native Americans, Levin and Campbell (N. Y.), replied later to some of the points in the report. Levin's speech was made in connection with a motion of his to amend a bill for raising a regiment of mounted riflemen by providing that the officers and soldiers should all be Americans by birth. He referred to what he called the effort to make it appear that the states possessed the power to create citizens of the United States. The Judiciary Committee's report had referred them to state laws for every right, civil and political, that an alien could possess. In fact, the federal system was purely political, and naturalization must confer rights purely political—suffrage and office-holding. The Constitution gave states the unquestionable right to decide on what terms *American citizens* could vote. But if they could grant to aliens suffrage for presidential electors, they could also grant eligibility to the presidency to aliens. No probation would be necessary if naturalization were designed only to confer rights relative to property, or other civil and personal rights of residents of states. If the states controlled the suffrage, and did not discriminate between aliens and citizens, no certificate of naturalization would be necessary, no record of alienage could be traced, and the functions of government would come entirely within the power of foreigners, in flagrant violation of the Constitution.   Changes in the period of probation showed conclusively that the great and fundamental right of naturalization was suffrage, and suffrage only.   Five or fourteen years' residence, knowledge, good character, were not required to hold property, fight, or act in civil relations.   The very idea of probation applied to the ballot box, and the practice, except in Illinois and Michigan, sustained this view.   The absurdity of the report on that point was self-evident.   It was absurd to prove the non-existence of a law by its violation.   If the states could admit aliens to vote, the Constitution was a dead letter.   If, as they were told, the denial of naturalization and the suffrage would create discontent, cabal and insurrection, they should exclude foreigners totally.   In twenty-one years all distinct interests, jealousy, and rivalry would cease, and the foreign party would be extinguished.   No other country on the globe admitted the foreigner, or even its own people, to rights of sovereignty.[38]

Campbell declared that alien voting in Michigan and Illinois was a plain violation of

[38] *Congressional Globe,* Twenty-ninth Congress, First Session, 605.

the spirit of the Constitution. The first constitution of New York (1777) gave the state power to pass general laws for naturalization, but the state never passed any such law, and passed only one special act naturalizing by name about one hundred persons. They had not thought it was wise to open wide the door to citizenship.[39]

The real question in dispute between Campbell and the committee was as to whether in making the Constitution a distinct federal citizenship was established, and the various state citizenships merged into it, to the extent at least of all of their political rights. In that case, unquestionably, the right of suffrage must be derived from this new citizenship, and could never be extended beyond it while the Constitution, in letter or in interpretation, remained unchanged and retained its controlling force.

In this view of the case, the federal citizenship from which suffrage derived attached to former state citizens by the adoption of the Constitution. Thereafter it could be gained only by birth or by naturalization. Birth anywhere within the United States wrought a uniform result in this respect, and the effect of birth abroad would be regulated by the

[39] *Loc. cit.*, 619.

federal naturalization laws. The power of naturalization was confided wholly to the general government. Thus the states no longer had anything to say as to who became citizens, while they had full control of the terms on which citizens could vote, subject only to the constitutional requirement that the citizens of each state have the privileges of citizens in the several states.

By the process described the idea of state citizenship must have lost so much of its content as to change its character or destroy it entirely. Two courses would remain by which the idea might survive in a limited sense. It might be applied to distinguish those federal citizens who resided in the state from other federal citizens, leaving all other persons in the state to be regarded as aliens from every point of view. In this case there would scarcely be contrast enough to support a very definite idea of two citizenships. Or its application might be extended to include unnaturalized foreigners in the exercise of certain rights secured to them through residence in the state, in which case the content of the idea would be reduced to the sum of those alien rights. State pride could be depended upon to prevent state citizenship from being reduced to mean so little, and the alternative would involve identifying it with federal citizenship.

But if the federal citizenship did not monopolize the suffrage power, and the states retained the right to make voters, of any grade at all, from aliens, the presumption would be easy and natural that they were not excluded from granting to aliens the suffrage for members of the lower house of the legislature. With that granted, nothing could prevent the entire federal suffrage from being given at the will of the state. That would give to state citizenship ample content, and the distinction between it and federal citizenship would be forced into prominence.

The constitutional provisions are that members of the House of Representatives shall be chosen "by the People of the several States," having "the Qualifications requisite for Electors of the most numerous Branch of the State Legislature;" and "Each State shall appoint in such manner as the Legislature thereof may direct, a Number of presidential Electors." The only restrictions are in the one case that the "State shall appoint," and in the other that elections shall be by "the People of the several States." If these terms were construed abstractly in the light of strong notions of allegiance, or of the con-

trast between aliens and citizens, they would
be found to warrant Campbell's conclusions;
but, when considered practically in a new
country, where aliens were numerous or settlers were greatly desired, and where ideas of
individual liberty had dethroned perpetual allegiance, foreigners would clearly be "People
of the several States." Perhaps nothing short
of an explicit exclusion, such as was made in
regard to the presidency, could have kept
them from the suffrage wherever the terms
of naturalization were thought to be harsh.

Levin spoke in the next Congress on a bill
intended to prevent the crowded condition
of emigrant ships. He was opposed to the
whole system of importing voters, and attributed it to party policy intended to weaken
the Native American party. He should move
to amend the title to, "A bill to accommodate
the paupers and criminals of Europe in their
migrations to the United States." The naturalization laws were obsolete in principle,
object, and tendency, and most destructive in
practice. They had been designed to adopt
a class of aliens qualified by morals, manners,
and education to aid in expanding the country
and consolidating the new government. But
Europe no longer drove out her valuable
and gifted sons—instead of them she was

sending over famine victims. He would feed them, but not rally to the polls that living mass of moral putrescence and pitiable ignorance. When the Native American vote equaled the foreign vote, the question would be settled.[40]

The question of pauper and criminal immigrants continued to be agitated throughout the Native American and Know-Nothing periods, and has begun to be solved only in much more recent times. Memorials brought the subject before both House and Senate in the spring of 1847. The Senate at length discharged its committee from consideration of it, but printed information from the secretary of state showed shipments of these classes from Switzerland and Germany, and probably of paupers from Ireland.[41] A bill was introduced in the House to prevent the importation of these classes, but it came to naught. In 1850 the New Orleans Board of Health petitioned Congress to tax alien passengers arriving in the United States. In response to this petition, the House Judiciary Committee reported a bill for such a tax, the pro-

[40] *Congressional Globe,* Twenty-ninth Congress, Second Session, Appendix, 385.

[41] (492) *Senate Journal,* Twenty-ninth Congress, Second Session, 232; (496) *House Journal,* 468; (499) *House Documents,* Twenty-ninth Congress, Second Session, No. 54.

ceeds to go to authorized state officers for eleemosynary purposes.[42]

In 1851-52 a number of petitions were referred in both houses, and again the Senate committee was discharged from considering them further.[43] In 1855 a resolution of the Rhode Island Legislature called for a law to prohibit the introduction of foreign paupers and criminals. It was sent to the governors of the other states for presentation to their legislatures as well as to Congress.[44] The Senate debated a resolution of inquiry calling upon the president for information as to the transportation of foreign convicts and paupers into the United States, and the agency of governments and municipal authorities therein; the voluntary immigration of those classes into the United States; and the legislation necessary. Cooper (Pa.), who introduced the resolution, said that friendly nations had no right to make of the United States a penal colony; yet there was scarcely an emigrant ship not freighted partly with

[42] (492) *Senate Journal,* Twenty-ninth Congress, Second Session, 158, 216; (495) *Senate Documents,* Twenty-ninth Congress, Second Session, No. 161.

[43] (610) *Senate Journal,* Thirty-second Congress, First Session, 42, 93, 117, 219, 225, 243, 274, 420, 436; (632) *House Journal,* Thirty-second Congress, First Session, 103, 237, 280, 292, 327, 385.

[44] (745) *Senate Journal,* Thirty-third Congress, Second Session, 293; (772) *Senate Miscellaneous Documents,* Thirty-third Congress, Second Session, No. 19.

that kind of cargo. The evil had lately alarmingly increased. One vessel in New York had recently landed one hundred and fifty paupers, and fifteen or sixteen convicts wearing chains. The Sardinian government had recently shipped thirty-four convicted criminals. Some years before two hundred and sixty Hessian convicts, a ship-load, came to Baltimore with manacles and fetters still on hands and feet. The mayor detained them and wrote the secretary of state, who replied that there was no law to prevent their landing. He gave figures to show that the foreign-born paupers in the United States in 1850 were over two thousand more than the paupers of native birth.

Brodhead replied that it was easier to make a speech than to introduce a bill to meet the difficulty that would be conformable to the Constitution. Cooper had not told the remedy.[45] The states had authority and had acted. New York taxed every foreigner, and exacted security from ship-owners that immigrants would not become a charge. Where was the jurisdiction in Congress? He was opposed to immigration, but did not know how to frame a bill not in conflict with state authority, state rights, and state jurisdic-

[45] Cooper replied that the resolution showed a practical purpose.

tion.[46] A little later, Jones (Tenn.) submitted a resolution for consideration, in substance as follows: *Whereas,* The Constitution confers on Congress the power to establish a uniform rule of naturalization, and is silent as to the exercise of any power over the subject of emigration; and *Whereas,* The Constitution declares that the powers not delegated to the United States nor prohibited to the states are reserved to the states or to the people; *Resolved,* That Congress has no power to pass any law regulating or controlling immigration into any states or territories. The power to establish necessary rules belongs to the states or to the people. Each state may determine for itself the evils arising from criminal and pauper immigration, and apply such remedy as its wisdom may suggest or its safety demand.[47]

In the House this question culminated in a struggle to secure the passage of a bill reported by Wentworth from the Committee on Commerce. Its opponents succeeded in holding it back until the very close of the session (March 3, 1855). Appeals were made to withdraw it, and charges that it had been sprung upon the House, although the bill had

[46] (745) *Senate Journal,* Thirty-third Congress, Second Session, 151, 164; *Congressional Globe,* Thirty-third Congress, Second Session, 388-91; January 25, 1855.

[47] *Congressional Globe,* Thirty-third Congress, Second Session, 783; February 17, 1855.

been in print for two months. Breckinridge would not discuss the question of the power of the general government to prevent states from allowing the entrance of such as they chose, but, assuming the power, there was a cruel exercise of it in the bill. It required every human being desirous of coming to the United States to procure a consul's certificate that he was not lunatic, poor, or blind, and had not been for five years. At first it had forbidden bringing the blind child in a man's family, but it had been patched up with an amendment so that it did not apply to a member of a family with sufficient property for its support. Any person who was the whole support of a family and was old, young, rich, or poor was repelled if blind. He wanted no property qualifications for residence in the United States. It was anti-American, anti-republican, and most odious. The provision to exclude as a pauper a person who had received aid within a year might exclude one as worthy as the man who had millions. He knew that the proscriptive feeling of which he regarded the bill as one of the fruits, was popular, and was sweeping like a hurricane from one end of the country to the other; but it conflicted with fundamental principles of the government, and he was willing to oppose it and await the reaction in public sentiment that he knew would come. Wentworth had been beaten by the Know-Nothing political society, and might have introduced that bill to extinguish Know-Nothingism.

I would rather trust to the next Congress, full of Know Nothings, as it is likely to be, to pass a bill upon this subject, than to take this bill, patched up and thrust upon us at this late period of the session, with a view to compromise the question.

Wentworth replied that the bill was started before he had much knowledge of the existence of the new ism. His state maintained two or three thousand foreign paupers. The whole seaboard was calling for the law. The Rhode Island Legislature and the New York Common Council favored it. The Emigrant Society of New York had been urging a much more restrictive bill, from which some additions to this were taken. The Supreme Court had decided that Congress had power to regulate the whole subject, and that the Massachusetts and New York restriction laws were unconstitutional and void; that Congress could control the introduction of foreigners, and that states had no right to legislate in any way to contravene their introduction or importation. The case of Gibbons and Ogden, and the passenger cases had settled the question. Any necessary legislation must come from Congress alone. The passenger laws since 1848 had been equally restrictive and penal. No property qualification was made; for if one were not a pauper, he could come without a farthing. To a request to state the constitutional clause under which power was claimed, he replied that it was claimed under a decision of the Supreme Court, and that there was no necessity of going into the constitutional argument. Breckinridge failed in an effort to get the floor to offer a substitute, and Hendricks again appealed to the House not to attempt to pass the bill at that late hour. It was laid on the table by a vote of 68 to 53.[48]

The next year [49] the House Committee on Foreign Relations reported back a bill to prevent the introduction into the United States of foreign criminals, paupers, idiots, lunatics, insane, and blind persons. In a long report the committee discussed the evils to be remedied, and asserted that both the general and state governments could do much to stay the tide of immigration of that undesirable population. The states generally had

[48] (709) *House Journal,* Thirty-third Congress, First Session, 1802; (776) *ibid.,* Second Session, 137, 139, 574, 582; *Congressional Globe,* Thirty-third Congress, Second Session, 158, 167, 174, 970, 1180-1187.

[49] August 16, 1856.

been as much remiss as Congress. Suggestions were made as to how they could enforce a truly American policy on all subjects. The bill did not get beyond the Committee of the Whole House on the State of the Union.[50]

Resolutions on this subject, one of them from the legislature of Maine, were before different Senate committees in 1857, and in the House in 1858; but nothing more important was done with them than the discharge of some committees having them in hand.[51]

In February, 1841, the Senate Committee on Judiciary reported a bill to declare the rights of children of citizens of the United States born abroad. The bill was considered and passed to third reading, but was then laid on the table.[52] In December, 1844, notice was given in the House of leave to be asked to introduce a similar bill.[53] The bill of the House Judiciary Committee of 1845, heretofore described, provided that such children should be deemed native.[54]

[50] (838) *House Journal*, Thirty-fourth Congress, First Session, 474, 631, (839) 1491; (870) *House Reports of Committees*, Thirty-fourth Congress, First and Second Sessions, 359.

[51] (917) *Senate Journal*, Thirty-fifth Congress, First Session, 49, 360, 364, 488; (934) *Senate Miscellaneous Documents*, Thirty-fifth Congress, First Session, No. 12; (940) *House Journal*, 131, 197.

[52] (374) *Senate Journal*, Twenty-sixth Congress, Second Session, 188, 214; February 17 and 27, 1841.

[53] (462) *House Journal*, Twenty-eighth Congress, Second Session, 104.

[54] See p. 244.

Three years later Webster was given leave to bring in a bill to extend the benefits of the naturalization law to the wives and children of citizens. The bill provided that all persons then or thereafter born out of the limits of the United States, of a father or mother being or having been a natural-born citizen of the United States, should be entitled to all the rights and privileges of citizenship; also that every woman married, or who should be married, to a citizen of the United States, should be deemed and taken to be a citizen. Webster explained that the bill had a very simple and important object. By the law of 1812, except by a violent construction of it, children born abroad of Americans resident or traveling there, were not to be deemed citizens. That act said "of parents who heretofore have been, or now are, citizens of the United States," but did not say "hereafter shall be." At the time he was speaking parents might be forty-six years old who were not born in 1802, and their children born abroad were excluded from citizenship by necessary construction of the act. Story, Kent, and others thought the act was very vaguely drawn. Though it was intended to apply to naturalized citizens, it could not be construed to do so. To remedy that, making the act apply to all citizens, was the main provision of the bill. The Judiciary Committee reported an amendment, that Webster indorsed as simplifying the measure. It then provided that the children of citizens of the United States, born out of the United States, should be considered as citizens, provided that the rights of citizenship should not descend to persons whose fathers never had been residents in the United States. By sec. 2 every woman married already or thereafter to a citizen of the United States, and continuing to reside in the United States, should be deemed and taken to be a citizen. The bill did not get out of the committee of the whole.[55] An item in *Niles Register*, March 30, 1844, was as follows:

ALIEN FEMALES. *An alien wife should be naturalized.* It was decided by Judge Kent in the New York circuit court, on Saturday, that a wife, born abroad, and not naturalized, could not inherit property devised to her by a husband.[56]

A bill similar to that of Webster passed two readings at the first session of the following Congress, and was read early in the second session, but has no further record;[57] and a

[55] (502) *Senate Journal,* Thirtieth Congress, First Session, 382, 390; *Congressional Globe,* Thirtieth Congress, First Session, 827, 834, 844; June 12, 13, 15, 1848.

[56] *Niles Register,* LXVI, 80.

[57] (566) *House Journal,* Thirty-first Congress, First Session, 284, 523; *Congressional Globe,* Thirty-first Congress, First Session, 24.

Senate bill with the same object was amended by the Senate Judiciary Committee in 1852.

At length the Thirty-third Congress succeeded in legislating upon these subjects by devoting to them some time at both sessions. The House and the Senate Judiciary Committees were each instructed, on the same day,[58] to inquire as to any necessary legislation to secure the rights of citizenship to children of American citizens born abroad. Seward submitted the resolution in the Senate. The House resolution had directed a report by bill or otherwise, at as early a day as possible. A bill was reported on January 13, and passed the same day.[59] Cutting explained for the committee that it was one eminently necessary to correct a lamentable defect in the law, and deserved immediate action. It provided that all persons born out of the United States, whose fathers [60] were citizens of the United States, should be deemed citizens, provided that the rights of citizenship should not descend to children whose fathers never resided in the United States. Any woman, not a citizen, when married to a citizen should be deemed a citizen. The act of 1790 had pro-

[58] December 20, 1853.

[59] (709) *House Journal,* Thirty-third Congress, First Session, 117, 199.

[60] Webster's bill had said "fathers or mothers."

vided for such children, but that of 1802 had left them aliens if their parents were born after 1802. The difficulty did not manifest itself for nearly fifty years; but was noticed some ten or twelve years before. The Senate bill of 1841 seemed to have been forgotten. A later House bill unfortunately went to the receptacle of all things that were to be lost— the Committee of the Whole House on the State of the Union. If this went there, the chances were against its being reached. The woman section was taken, nearly in exact words, from the English act of 1844. There could be no objection to it, because women possessed no political rights. There was no good reason for putting women to the probationary term, and the trouble and expense of naturalization. Being a citizen, she would train her children properly. New York had passed special acts for five or six years past to guard against escheat of property that should descend to certain children born abroad, but the state could not regulate their political rights. An effort to refer this bill to the committee of the whole, in the interest of other desired amendments to the naturalization law, failed.[61]

In the Senate petitions against its passage

[61] *Congressional Globe,* Thirty-third Congress, First Session, 169; January 13, 1854.

without amendment were received,[62] and Seward soon after presented other petitions against the passage of the bill.[63] Apparently it was the second section, providing that an alien woman, when married to a citizen, should become a citizen, that had prevented action on the subject before, and that caused the opposition of the petitioners. The Senate Judiciary Committee recommended that this section be struck out. Nearly a year later, Bayard explained that the committee had revised its opinion, and he was instructed by it to propose, instead of its former amendment, to insert after "woman" the words "who might be lawfully naturalized under existing laws." He said that it was considered both necessary and proper that the wife should not become a citizen unless she could be naturalized under existing laws.[64] The bill passed with this amendment, and the House accepted it after placing "lawfully" before instead of after "be." [65]

The amendment would prevent the citizenship of negro, Indian, or Chinese women. It

[62] One of these was from "Horatio Seymour and others."

[63] (689) *Senate Journal,* Thirty-third Congress, First Session, 53, 119, 130, 170.

[64] *Congressional Globe,* Thirty-third Congress, Second Session, 92; December 20, 1854.

[65] *Ibid.,* 632.

seems to require moral character and attachment to the principles of the Constitution.
Perhaps it is an open question whether five
years' residence is also required by it. The
bill became a law on February 10, 1855.

CHAPTER XIV

THE KNOW-NOTHING PERIOD

Returning to the agitation for twenty-one years' residence as a prerequisite to naturalization, note at the outset that petitions do not assume the importance henceforth that they did in the earlier Native American movement. Party lines are more tightly drawn, and there is little use of asking political opponents for votes in Congress.

On January 23, 1850, Levin gave notice of a bill for the protection of the ballot box by an extension of the naturalization law to twenty-one years and by a capitation tax.[1] This was perhaps the last act in the old agitation. The new began at the opening of the second session of the Thirty-third Congress in December, 1854, when Taylor (Tenn.) in the House, and Adams (Miss.) in the Senate, gave notice of bills, the one to repeal or modify the naturalization laws, and the other to amend the Naturalization Act of 1802. Taylor's bill was introduced by unanimous consent, but did not get out of the hands of the Judiciary Committee.[2] The Senate bill met

[1] *Congressional Globe*, Thirty-first Congress, First Session, 219.
[2] (776) *House Journal*, Thirty-third Congress, Second Session, 40, 259.

a similar fate, but Adams made a speech upon
it before it was referred. He explained that
the twenty-one years' residence to be required
was entirely prospective. All inhabitants of
the United States at the time of the passage
of the bill were to have the benefit of the
existing law. He gave the growth of the
population since 1800 as about 33 per cent.
every ten years. At that rate they would
number about 101,000,000 by 1900. The
natives would need the whole country, but immigration was increasing alarmingly. He referred to riots and mobs, the recent hanging
of an American senator in effigy,[3] and the
formation of the German Progressive Republican Party, with one of its objects to abolish
the sabbath. If five years had been a proper
time in 1802 for the "then" class of immigrants (only seven thousand a year, and scat-
tered) to become acquainted with the government, twenty-one years was not too long for
the class of people coming now, three hundred and seventy thousand a year, in large
bands, settling whole neighborhoods and com-
munities, and keeping their own language.
He believed that public opinion demanded
the proposed change, and the safety of the
government required it. The new party had

[3] Douglas, chairman of the committee on territories, had been
hanged in effigy by foreigners, called a German mob.

had great success in the last election. He did not belong to the Know-Nothing organization, and had twice advocated similar views in the House before its successes were made, when he had favored the entire repeal of the naturalization laws. He was told that states possessed and exercised control over the suffrage. His answer was that the states, having conferred the right of naturalization on the general government, should, in all good faith to the general government and to each other, conform the qualifications of voters to the laws of naturalization. Many of them had done so, and recent changes in public opinion justified the belief that nearly all would conform to the principles of his bill. He was not tenacious about twenty-one years, but thought it the proper and favorite time. No man in the United States could complain of injustice by the bill.[4] A petition was received from the Rhode Island Legislature,[5] asking, among other things, for a new naturalization law requiring twenty-one years' continuous residence, and that all processes and oaths be taken in a United States circuit or district court, and before the judge in open court.

[4] *Congressional Globe,* Thirty-third Congress, Second Session, 15, 24-26.

[5] See p. 265.

This was laid on the table by the Senate,[6] and referred by the House.[7]

A number of speeches, *pro* and *con,* on Know-Nothingism were made during this session of Congress. N. P. Banks defended the right of the Know-Nothings to organize secretly. Their object made such organization a popular movement and not a conspiracy. He stated that the ground of their opposition to Roman Catholic naturalization was that their allegiance was claimed by the pope. There had been great growth in immigration, and Old World conditions would increase it. Chinese immigration to Japan had been limited; many Chinese were already in California. With steamers crossing the Pacific in ten or twelve days, who could prophesy its outcome? Or who could check it? The Supreme Court had decided that the states could not. If they came, they would be admitted. Should they be naturalized in five years? An organized minority of foreign-born had great power, for which there was no remedy except that union that was understood to be a chief object of the Know-Nothings. A change in the naturalization laws would not remedy

[6] (745) *Senate Journal,* Thirty-third Congress, Second Session, 293; (772) *Senate Miscellaneous Documents,* Thirty-third Congress, Second Session, No. 19.

[7] (776) *House Journal,* Thirty-third Congress, Second Session, 423; February 21, 1855.

that evil. Yet extending the term of residence required, and more stringent execution of the laws, might be justified. Whether the term should be twenty-one, twelve, or ten years he would leave for others to say.[8]

Barry (Miss.) said that the Know-Nothing purposes were unknown—as set forth they were contradictory. Prejudice and hostility to foreigners were greater inversely as the degree of civilization of a nation. The Know-Nothings sought to justify themselves by claiming that there are secret foreign organizations, but these they dignify by imitating. Know-Nothing purposes seem to be: (1) the exclusion of all foreigners from office; (2) the extension of the naturalization law to twenty-one years or other period; (3) the entire repeal of naturalization laws; (4) the exclusion of Roman Catholics from office. The real danger was in foreigners congregating alone, and proscription tended to cause that. They might even get complete control of some northwestern state. He admitted the duty of excluding paupers and criminals. If the evil from them was as great as was charged, it was remarkable that they had been allowed to come so long. If the naturalization laws were repealed, the states would

[8] *Congressional Globe,* Appendix, Thirty-third Congress, Second Session, 49-52; December 18, 1854.

then legislate. Naturalization gave nearly all rights, and yet the states could bestow nearly all without naturalization. They gave full suffrage, holding real estate, and state office. Other states did not recognize these rights, and a law of Congress was necessary to give the privileges and immunities of citizens in the several states. A state could even deny suffrage to all who were not natives of it. Not a voter in the Union derived his power from the federal government.[9] His state (Miss.) had one foreigner to sixty population, while some states had one to eight or ten. The problem differed, and states dealt with it as they found it. This movement at the North was a combination of all the isms— abolitionism, free-soilism, Whig-, woman's rights-, social-, and anti-rent*ism*. Seward was against Know-Nothingism, for he had committed himself against foreign voters, and he had sagacity. It was the universal opinion in political circles that the movement was for a brief day. The discordant elements would dissolve it, if no other causes did. This new ism was the old alien law and Native Americanism. The old unlaid spirit of federalism was abroad. It was hostile to democracy.[10]

[9] This would need qualification as to inhabitants of territories.

[10] *Congressional Globe,* Appendix, Thirty-third Congress, Second Session, 53.

Sollers (Md.), a pro-slavery southerner, defended Know-Nothingism. The immigration, only one hundred and twenty thousand for the first twenty years, had swelled to an ocean stream that would sweep away government, laws, institutions, and the very name of American. Its character also had totally changed. It was the domestic policy of foreign governments to send over the refuse of their jails and prisons, and their paupers also. As to Know-Nothing secrecy, the Boston Tea Party was secret, and he held in his hand at that moment a call for a secret Democratic caucus. He denied that the principles of the Native American party were secret. Also, it warred against no religion, but against the union of church and state, against the mingling of religion with politics, and against allegiance to a foreign prince or potentate combined with American citizenship. He denied that Know-Nothingism had first appeared in the House in the person of Banks, of Massachusetts—he himself had first introduced a proposition to exclude foreigners from the army and navy. Look at the victories of the party. It had swept over Pennsylvania like a whirlwind, and failed in New York only because it knew not its own strength. It was victorious in New Jersey

and Delaware. In Massachusetts it had an-
nihilated all its opponents. He could not
doubt its triumphant success, and that none
but "Americans shall govern America." [11]

W. R. Smith (Ala.) referred to propositions in both houses to repeal or modify the
naturalization laws. It was becoming the
great question of the age. The voice of the
people would force the legislatures to take a
stand, and all mere party organizations would
have to retire before it. The vituperations
of the press were leveled against the movement, but he felt no apprehensions. They
presented the simple proposition—the purifi-
cation of the ballot box; and proposed only
to exclude unnaturalized foreigners, and to
check immigration by wholesome laws. They
had some radical propositions, but no bill, because nobody could suppose that that Congress would favor this reformation. They
could not expect that an administration so
distinctly committed in favor of foreigners
and foreign influence as the existing one
would take the back track. He did not suppose that the bill before them would receive
any serious attention. There was no law to exclude a foreigner, and no effectively administered one requiring a passport. No other coun-

[11] *Loc. cit.*, 83.

try on earth was so situated. No immigrant should land without taking a solemn oath renouncing allegiance to all foreign powers and declaring *bona fide* intention to become an inhabitant of the United States. A passport from a consul should be required, and both captain and passport should inform him of the requirements here. England, France, Russia, and all governments in the East required a passport. A foreign power could land on their shores any number of soldiers before committing any hostile act. How easy it would be for Russia to land a hundred thousand in a month, and they could equip themselves after landing! Consuls should investigate and give passports only to suitable persons. A modification of the naturalization laws should prevent all foreigners from voting who were not naturalized already or had not taken steps to become so, except that boys under ten, or even fifteen, immigrating with their parents, should be considered citizens in every respect at the age of twenty-one. There had been fraud, negligence, and corruption from the foundation of the government in the administration of the naturalization laws. Of three hundred thousand immigrants landed in New York alone during 1854 only five thousand applied for naturalization or swore allegiance to the country. In five years more there would be a million a year coming. There was no law to prevent a pagan Chinese from appearing in Congress with power to mingle in its councils.[12]

L. M. Keitt (S. C.) said that the country had recently been amazed by the successes of a novel political organization which disparaged the dignity of American character by threatening it with subjection to a secret order. It was argued that the power to naturalize enabled Congress to regulate the constituency. But for what did Congress make a citizen of the United States? The Constitution answered: The citizens of each state shall be entitled to all the privileges and immunities of the citizens in the several states. Since many states affixed a property qualification, and perhaps all required a term of residence, how could privileges and immunities refer to the right to vote? They referred to property and personal rights, and not political. The discussion in the convention had shown a clear purpose to leave the control of suffrage to the states. The Know-Nothing movement looked to the consolidation of

12 *Loc. cit.*, 94. The last statement would be true only of a naturalized Chinaman, twelve years a resident. The question of naturalizing Chinese was an unsettled one then, or one hardly yet raised.

the government; and, if consolidated, he asked: Was it then worth preserving?[13]

Witte moved a suspension of the rules that he might offer resolutions that the existence of such a secret, oath-bound political organization was inconsistent with republican institutions and hostile to the genius of the government. The attempt to proscribe citizens for religion, or to favor or injure a religious denomination, was a direct violation of the spirit of the Constitution. Careful and strict administration of the naturalization laws was a solemn duty; yet interference with the rights of naturalized citizens was inconsistent with the plighted faith of the nation, and must diminish its growth and prosperity. The vote on this motion was 104 to 78, lacking eighteen of the necessary two-thirds.[14] Three similar resolutions were proposed in the Senate shortly before,[15] but were dropped without being acted upon.[16] Opposition was further shown by a resolution of the Legislature of Wisconsin, presented by Senator Dodge, declaring that they were opposed to any altera-

[13] *Congressional Globe,* Appendix, Thirty-third Congress, Second Session, 66.

[14] (776) *House Journal,* Thirty-third Congress, Second Session, 314.

[15] January 25, 1855.

[16] *Congressional Globe,* Thirty-third Congress, Second Session, 391.

tion of the naturalization laws, and directing their members to oppose any law extending the time of residence for naturalization.[17]

The prolonged contest over the speakership in the House in 1855, and the presidential campaign of 1856, each caused debates in which political parties and Know-Nothingism were much discussed. In the speakership contest, Cox (Ky.) said that he considered none to be Americans who did not accept the twelfth section of the Philadelphia platform. All others were apostates or bolters. The American Council had declared that agitation of slavery was not a question of importance in the order—that it was not a question at all. This was an expression of the intention of the party to be national, to abide by existing laws, and to throw out of Congress all agitation on that subject for the future.[18]

[17] (745) *Senate Journal,* Thirty-third Congress, Second Session, 231; (772) *Senate Miscellaneous Documents,* Thirty-third Congress, Second Session, No. 12.

[18] The section referred to, adopted at Philadelphia, June, 1855, was in part as follows: "The National Council has deemed it the best guarantee of common justice and future peace, to abide by and maintain the existing laws on the subject of slavery, as a final and conclusive settlement of that subject in spirit and in substance." It further declared that Congress had no power to legislate upon the subject in the states, or to exclude any state because its constitution did or did not recognize slavery; and that Congress ought not to legislate upon the subject in the territories nor interfere with it in the District of Columbia. The new platform adopted in February, 1856, made no mention of slavery. It was asserted in Congress that Fillmore would not have accepted the presidential nomination on the former platform (*Congressional Globe,* Thirty-fourth Congress, First Session, Appendix, 1152).

The position taken by the Democratic party on that question was identical with that of the Americans. He wished to make a gulf impassable between Americans and abolitionists. The Democratic members of the House had passed a resolution, which he quoted, giving congratulations on the triumph in various places of the doctrines of civil and religious liberty which had been so violently assailed by a secret order, known as the Know-Nothing party. The position of the administration and these resolutions of the Democratic caucus disabled the Americans from bringing support to elect a Democratic speaker. He could not carry with him enough Native Americans to elect a Democrat if he would; but let the Democrats come to the Americans, and they would elect a speaker and defeat northern sectionalism. The American party wanted no disturbing legislation; it asked only for peace.[19]

Some time after the election of Banks as speaker, Smith (Tenn.) read the names of 120 out of 234 members of the House, whom he declared to have been elected as Know-Nothings or Americans. He called all who had received Know-Nothing support Know-Nothings, and said that they were elected by Know-Nothings. Seventy-five of them, he

[19] *Congressional Globe,* Appendix, Thirty-fourth Congress, First Session, 34-41; December 21, 1855.

said, had voted for Banks, who had been the
champion of their order in Congress.
Twenty-eight abolitionists had voted for him,
and not a Democrat.[20]   Elliott said that the
Know-Nothings had carried a majority of
the House, thirty from the South and ninety
from the North, according to the undenied
count of Smith, of Tennessee, and then had
permitted the election of Banks.   The war
on the Democratic party by southern Know-
Nothings was much fiercer than that on the
Black Republican, or northern wing of their
party.[21]

Marshall (Ill.) said:

Another wing of this allied army engaged in unholy
warfare against the Democratic party is the southern
branch of the Know Nothing party; the northern branch,
with very few exceptions, having been swallowed up and
completely identified with the Black Republican movement.

Born of bigotry and intolerance, that secret,
oath-bound organization had sprung up full-
grown in a night time for a brief career; with
the frosts of November it would have passed
from the earth. The blackest page in the history of those times would be the record of
ingratitude of the Southern Know-Nothings
to the northern Democratic party.   The great

[20] *Ibid.*, 352; April 4, 1856.
[21] *Ibid.*, 1152.

abolition sea had swelled and rolled—these men had battled against it in the face of ostracism; but from Maine to California not one Know-Nothing member had been on the side of the Constitution in the contest.[22]

Talbott (Ky.), in showing that the Know-Nothing proposition that no state or territory should give the suffrage to unnaturalized foreigners was impracticable and unconstitutional, quoted from a speech of Hon. Garret Davis, "one of the ablest jurists of Kentucky," in the Kentucky constitutional convention. Davis had no doubt of the competency, the right, and the duty if for good, of Kentucky to require twenty-one years' residence for suffrage. It appeared to him wholly fallacious and untenable that states could not add to the requirements of the naturalization law of Congress for suffrage. The states could confer the elective franchise upon foreigners and make them eligible to office before naturalization; and they had undoubted power to exclude them after naturalization. Their citizenship conferred upon them only rights conceded by the federal Constitution, and not a single one under any state government. States could wholly deny both suffrage and office to naturalized per-

22 *Loc. cit.*, 1228.

sons, or could confer both fully or with restrictions as they would. Talbott added that
nearly half of the states allowed foreigners
to vote in from nine months to two years.
Power in Congress over the suffrage by naturalization meant power to control property,
age, and other qualifications for suffrage.[23]

In February, 1856, Adams (Miss.), whose
naturalization bill had been suppressed in a
Senate Committee, in the previous Congress,[24] introduced a new bill.[25] It provided
that no alien arriving after its passage should
become a citizen, unless on his application
he should declare on oath, and prove to the
satisfaction of the court, twenty-one years'
continuous residence in the United States.
Declaration of intention should not be permitted until the alien had resided at least ten
years in the United States. Any alien free
white person, having proved twelve months'
residence in the United States, should be

entitled to all the protection of the government, and be
allowed to inherit, and hold, and transmit real estate, so
long as he remains within the limits of the United States,
in the same manner as though he were a citizen.[26]

[23] *Ibid.,* 1233; July 28, 1856.

[24] See p. 278.

[25] (809) *Senate Journal,* Thirty-fourth Congress, First Session,
84.

[26] Quoted from a summary of the bill.

Aliens should be admitted only in a United States circuit or district court in some state or territory. The penalty was to be five hundred dollars for a ship bringing in any immigrant without an authenticated consular certificate, deposited with the master, that the person was of good character, had never been convicted of a criminal offense, and never had been a pauper.[27] Toombs, from the Judiciary Committee, returned the bill without amendment, but with the report that it ought not to pass.

Several special orders were made for its consideration in committee of the whole, to accommodate Adams, who finally made a two-hour speech upon it. It appears that no one else cared to discuss it,[28] and nothing more was done with it. Adams said that, as mercy at the expense of justice became cruelty, so liberality to aliens at the expense of the morals, security, and rights of citizens was inexcusable, if not suicidal. He quoted largely to show opinions and abuses. Twenty years would double the population without immigration, and it would then be as dense as was consistent with their welfare. He was told that they would take Mexico when they

[27] *Congressional Globe,* Thirty-fourth Congress, First Session, 979; April 21, 1856.

[28] *Ibid.,* 1414.

needed more room, but he was opposed to a
deliberate plan to supply by robbery and mur-
der wants created by a permanent policy of
inviting the hordes of Europe to come and
partake of the bounty derived from their ancestors. Except for immigration, the South
would have gained upon the North in influence in Congress. Already five state legislatures had nullified a constitutional law of
Congress.[29] Division and anarchy were inevitable unless they checked immigration. He
was told there was no danger, as the immigrants voted the Democratic ticket. But let
them crush out the American party, as it was
said the next election would do, and, with the
contest between Republicans and Democrats,
how would the northern foreigners vote?
Seward, Giddings, and Greeley could tell
them. Nine-tenths of them would vote the
Republican ticket, for their whole education
and prejudices were against slavery.[30]

A year later a bill was introduced in the
House by Whitney to establish a uniform rule
of naturalization, and for the repeal of existing laws. Late in the summer [31] the Judiciary

[29] This probably refers to the passage of personal liberty laws
in the North.

[30] (809) *Senate Journal,* Thirty-fourth Congress, First Session,
269, 319, 372, 381; *Congressional Globe,* Thirty-fourth Congress,
First Session, 1409f.

[31] July 21, 1856.

Committee reported it, with an amendment in the nature of a substitute. Hoffman, a Know-Nothing member from Maryland, made a speech upon it. In the next regular session, in December, a motion to discharge the committee of the whole from its further consideration, and instruct that it be reported to the House and made a special order from day to day until it was disposed of, was lost by a vote of 89 to 92.[32]

Hoffman referred to three dangerous measures that had recently passed. In spite of public sentiment, he said, the administration had brought forward a bill whose whole object was to open the floodgates wider to a stream of corruption and commerce in foreign merchantable votes, and to break down the guards against it. After days of struggle, a fusion of administration and abolition forces had transferred the capital city government from American to foreign hands. The District being the only place outside of the territories where Congress could regulate the suffrage, the bill was of great magnitude as regarded principle, line of policy, and precedent. Again, an amendment to the bill for a convention for organizing Oregon Terri-

[32] A two-thirds vote was necessary to carry. (838) *House Journal,* Thirty-fourth Congress, First Session, 489, 668; (839) 1250.

tory, by which suffrage was to be limited to citizens of the United States, had been rejected by fusion No. 2. Finally, when the Senate had passed the Kansas pacification bill, containing a repeal of the permission in the Kansas organic act for full suffrage and office-holding to unnaturalized foreigners, a majority of the Democrats had fused with the abolitionists against it. This was a gigantic stride toward denationalization.

The bill before them, while not all that was desired, had several leading provisions that were salutary. The period of probation was left blank, but a majority of the committee was for not less than seven years. As was eminently wise and proper, the bill provided for a registry law. Commencement of residence could be indicated by filing a statement with the clerk of the court, with ages and other particulars of self and family. Then the final petition for admission was to be filed at least twenty days before the commencement of the term of court, and no hearing on an application could be had within twenty days before an election. It would be well also to enact that no person or committee should pay the costs for the person naturalized. The greatest statesmen had acknowledged the necessity of a change in the existing system. The bill would destroy the business of putting through raw material even on election day.[33]

Meanwhile, a resolution of the Massachusetts Legislature was laid on the table in the House and referred in the Senate. It urged that their peculiar system, very distinct in spirit and principles, presupposed a state of society and public opinion never yet existing elsewhere. Republican institutions were especially adapted to an educated and intelligent people, capable of, and accustomed to, self-government. Free institutions could be confined safely only to free men—to men free from ignorance, and personal, religious, and political despotism. Foreigners could have in general, no sober appreciation of the principles, character, and purpose of such institutions. Aliens were, as a rule, incapable of exercising the franchise with advantage to themselves or with safety to others. The legislature recommended these truths to the consideration of the Massachusetts delegation in Congress; and requested their endeavors to extend the term of residence required for political rights, and their influence to place the offices of government, both at home and abroad, exclusively in the

[33] *Congressional Globe,* Thirty-fourth Congress, First Session, Appendix, 1212.

hands of native-born citizens who were opposed to every kind of despotism.[34]

In the House in January, 1857, Henry Winter Davis said that the recent election had developed in aggravated form every evil against which the American party protested. Republicans and Democrats had rivaled each other in bidding for the foreign vote. Foreign allies, men naturalized in thousands on the eve of election, had been struggled for by the competing parties. It was the high mission of the American party to restore the influence of the interests of the people. He called on the Americans of the North to return from the paths of error to the sound position of the American party, that of silence on the slavery agitation.[35]

Several hopeless efforts to amend the naturalization laws were made in the House from 1857 to 1860. A bill by Humphrey Marshall reached the Judiciary Committee.[36] Notice for leave to introduce bills was given by Marshall and I. N. Morris. Marshall also sought to introduce a joint resolution to

[34] (838) *House Journal,* Thirty-fourth Congress, First Session, 653; (809) *Senate Journal,* Thirty-fourth Congress, First Session, 114; *House Miscellaneous Documents,* Thirty-fourth Congress, First Session, March 7, 1856.

[35] *Congressional Globe,* Thirty-fourth Congress, Third Session, Appendix, 125.

[36] (892) *House Journal,* Thirty-fourth Congress, Third Session, 251.

amend the Constitution.[37] Finally, a bill by Morris, to amend the naturalization laws, was reported by Houston from the Judiciary Committee, with the recommendation, that it do not pass; and it was laid on the table.[38] Then came the Civil War, and the end of the American party.

[37] (940) *loc cit.*, Thirty-fifth Congress, First Session, 186, 1045.

[38] (995) *ibid.*, Thirty-fifth Congress, Second Session, 115, 260; *Congressional Globe,* Thirty-fifth Congress, Second Session, 611; January 26, 1859.

BIBLIOGRAPHY

ADAMS, HENRY. *History of the United States of America.* 9 vols. New York, 1889-91.

—— *Writings of Albert Gallatin.* 3 vols. Philadelphia, 1879.

ADAMS, JOHN QUINCY. *Memoirs of John Quincy Adams.* Edited by CHARLES FRANCIS ADAMS. 12 vols. Philadelphia, 1874.

ADAMS, JOHN. *The Works of John Adams.* With a Life of the Author by his grandson, CHARLES FRANCIS ADAMS. 10 vols. Boston, 1856.

American Historical Association, Papers and Annual Reports.

American State Papers. Documents, Legislative and Executive. Folio, 38 vols. Washington: Gales & Seaton, 1832-61.

Annals of Congress.

Aurora.

BANCROFT, GEORGE. *History of the Formation of the Constitution of the United States of America.* 2 vols. New York, 1882.

—— *History of the United States of America.* The author's last revision. 6 vols. New York, 1885.

BASSETT, JOHN SPENCER. *Slavery and Servitude in the Colony of North Carolina.* Johns Hopkins University Studies, Vol. XIV, Nos. 4, 5. Baltimore, 1896.

BEAULIEU, PAUL LEROY. *The Modern State in Relation to Society and the Individual.* London, 1891.

BLUNTSCHLI, J. K. *The Theory of the State.* Oxford, 1885.

BURGESS, JOHN W. *Political Science and Comparative Constitutional Law.* 2 vols. Boston, 1890.

CALHOUN, JOHN C. *Works.* 6 vols. New York, 1853–85.
Columbia College Studies in History.
CONWAY, MONCURE D. *Life of Thomas Paine.* 2 vols.
New York, 1892.
Congressional Globe.
Congressional Record.
CURTIS, GEORGE TICKNOR. *Constitutional History of the
United States.* Edited by JOSEPH CULBERTSON CLAYTON.
2 vols. New York, 1889–96.
DALLAS, A. J. *Life and Writings of Alexander James
Dallas.* By his son GEORGE M. DALLAS. Philadelphia,
1871.
Elliott's Debates.
English Statutes at Large.
Federalist, The. Edited by HENRY CABOT LODGE. New
York and London, 1895.
FRANKLIN, BENJAMIN. *The Works of Benjamin Franklin.*
With a Life of the Author by JARED SPARKS. 10 vols.
Boston, 1856.
FREEMAN, EDWARD A. *Comparative Politics.* London,
1873.
GALLATIN, ALBERT. *Writings.* Edited by HENRY ADAMS.
3 vols. Philadelphia, 1879.
HALL, W. E. *A Treatise on International Law.* Oxford,
1895.
HAMILTON, ALEXANDER. *The Works of Alexander Hamil-
ton.* Edited by HENRY CABOT LODGE. New York and
London, 1885.
HAMILTON, JOHN C. *History of the Republic of the United
States of America, as Traced in the Writings of Alex-
ander Hamilton and of His Cotemporaries.* Phila-
delphia, 1864.
HARRISON, FREDERIC. *Order and Progress.* London, 1875.
HENING, WILLIAM WALLER. *Statutes-at-Large; Being a*

Collection of All the Laws of Virginia (1619–1792).
13 vols. Philadelphia and New York, 1823.

HILDRETH, RICHARD. *History of the United States.* 6 vols.
New York, 1851–56.

HOLST, DR. H. VON. *The Constitutional and Political History of the United States.* 8 vols. Chicago, 1876–92.

House Documents.

House Executive Documents.

House Journals.

House Miscellaneous Documents.

House Reports of Committees.

HUNT, GAILLARD. *The American Passport.* Department
of State, Washington, 1898.

JAY, JOHN. *The Correspondence and Public Papers of
John Jay.* Edited by HENRY P. JOHNSON. 4 vols. New
York and London, 1893.

JEFFERSON, THOMAS. *The Writings of Thomas Jefferson.*
Edited by PAUL LEICESTER FORD. 10 vols. New York,
1892–99.

Johns Hopkins University Publications.

Journals of Congress. Printed by John Dunlap. Yorktown. 1778.

Kentucky Palladium.

KING, RUFUS. *Life and Correspondence of Rufus King.*
Edited by his grandson, CHARLES R. KING, M. D. 5
vols. New York, 1894.

LALOR, JOHN J., editor. *Cyclopedia of Political Science,
Political Economy, and of the Political History of the
United States.* 3 vols. Chicago, 1881–84.

LEWIS, SIR GEORGE CORNEWALL. *An Essay on the Government of Dependencies.* Oxford, 1891.

LOCKE, JOHN. *Two Treatises on Civil Government.* With
an Introduction by HENRY MORLEY. London, 1887.

LOWELL. *The Hessians in the Revolution.*

MACLAY, WILLIAM. *Journal of William Maclay, United States Senator from Pennsylvania, 1789–1791.* New York, 1890.

MACMASTER, JOHN BACH. *A History of the People of the United States.* 5 vols. New York, 1883–99.

MADISON, JAMES. *Letters and Other Writings of James Madison.* 4 vols. Philadelphia, 1865.

———— *The Papers of James Madison.* 3 vols. Washington, 1840.

Nation, The. New York, 1865—.

National Intelligencer.

New England Palladium.

New York Daily Express, 1838.

Niles Register. Baltimore, 1811–49.

Philadelphia Advertiser.

Political Science Quarterly. New York, 1886—.

POORE, BEN. PERLEY, compiler. *The Federal and State Constitutions, Colonial Charters, and Other Organic Laws of the United States.* 2 parts. Washington: Government Printing Office, 1877.

Register of Debates in Congress.

RHODES, JAMES FORD. *History of the United States from the Compromise of 1850.* 4 vols. New York, 1893–99.

SCHOULER, JAMES. *History of the United States of America.* 6 vols. New York, 1894.

Secret Journals of the Acts and Proceedings of Congress. 4 vols. Boston, 1821.

Senate Documents.

Senate Executive Documents.

Senate Journals.

Senate Reports of Committees.

SEWARD, WILLIAM H. *The Works of William H. Seward.* Edited by GEORGE E. BAKER. 5 vols. Boston, 1884.

SNOW, FREEMAN. *Treaties and Topics in American Diplomacy.* Boston, 1894.

—— *Cases and Opinions on International Law.* Boston, 1893.

South Carolina Gazette.

The Statutes at Large of the United States of America.

TAYLOR, HANNIS. *The Origin and Growth of the English Constitution.* Boston, 1889.

THORPE, FRANCIS NEWTON. *A Constitutional History of the American People, 1776–1850.* 2 vols. New York, 1898.

TODD, C. B. *Life and Letters of Joel Barlow.*

Treaties and Conventions Concluded between the United States and Other Powers since July 4, 1776. Washington, 1889.

United States Supreme Court Reports.

Virginia Magazine of History and Biography. Richmond, 1893—.

Washington Federalist.

WASHINGTON, GEORGE. *The Writings of George Washington.* Edited by WORTHINGTON CHAUNCEY FORD. 14 vols. New York and London, 1889.

WEBSTER, PRENTISS. *A Treatise on the Law of Citizenship in the United States.* Albany, N. Y., 1891.

—— *Law of Naturalization in the United States of America and of Other Countries.* Boston, 1895.

WHEATON. *History of the Law of Nations.*

WILSON, WOODROW. *The State.* Boston, 1889.

WOOLSEY, THEODORE D. *Political Science; or, The State Theoretically and Practically Considered.* New York, 1886.

INDEX

Act concerning evidence, 219f.
Act of 1790, 33 f., 48.
Act of 1795, 49 f., 70.
Act of 1798, 72 f.
Act of 1802, 97 f.
Act of 1813, 117 f.
Act of 1816, 129 f.
Act of 1824, 167 f.
Act of 1828, 178 f.
Adams, John, 8, 72.
Adams, J. Q., 9 f., 161 f., 165, 177, 206, 217, 219 f.
Alien enemies, 117–28.
Alien landholding, 33, 35, 37, 39, 42, 54, 66, 182, 254, 293.
Aliens, 73 f., 170 f., 176, 181 f., 212, 294.
Amendment to the Constitution, 147, 300.
Bancroft, George, 5, 15.
Banks, N. P., 281.
Bibliography, 301.
Buchanan, James, 178, 215.
Calhoun, John C., 132f., 161f.
Certificates, 130, 178 f., 228, 234, 245.
Children born abroad, 271 f.
Cicero, 139, 146.
Citizenship, 2, 4 f., 9 f., 14, 67, 76, 78 f., 260 f.; state, 93, 260 f.
Clay, Henry, 151.
Codification, 131, 181, 242.
Committee: of Detail, 21, 26, 30; on Style, 21, 30.
Confederation, Articles of, 12 f., 31.
Congress: Continental, 1, 2, 5, 8; Confederation, 13.
Constitution, 32.

Convention, Constitutional, 19 f.
Criminals, 193 f., 221, 226, 263 f.
Declaration of Independence, 1 f., 149, 241.
Declaration of Intention, 167 f., 175, 176, 180, 244, 293.
Dicey, Professor, 10 f.
District of Columbia, 296.
Douglas, Stephen A., 254.
Evidence, act concerning, 129 f.
Expatriation, 50, 54 f., 115 f., 120, 134 f., 241 f.
Federalist, 14.
France, 146.
Franklin, Benjamin, 12, 28 f.
Gallatin, Albert, 83, 87.
Giddings, Joshua R., 249.
Great Britain, 9, 141, 143, 153, 164, 186 f.
Hamilton, Alexander, 3, 22, 98–105.
Harrison, William Henry, 203 f.
Hessians, 5 f.
Immigration, 23, 38, 81, 167, 184 f., 264 f., 279, 286, 295.
Intercitizenship, 9 f., 12 f.
Investigations, 227.
Jefferson, Thomas, 6, 97 f., 134 f.
Kansas, 297.
Know-Nothings, 278 f. (See also Native Americanism.)
Levin, Mr., 248, 258, 263, 278.
Loughborough, Lord, 9.

Louisiana, 207.
Maclay's Journal, 43 f.
Madison, James, 14, 18f., 23f.,
    27, 30, 36, 40, 49, 53 f., 57,
    59, 61, 63, 118, 119.
Massachusetts, 188, 247, 269,
    298.
Michigan, 163 f.
Minors, 167, 202, 237, 244,
    286.
Missouri, 206.
Moral character, 53.
Native Americanism, 184 f.,
    255, 269; national conven-
    tion of, 247; Philadelphia
    platform of, 289. (See
    also Know-Nothings.)
Native citizens, 131 f., 258,
    271, 299.
Naturalization: by England,
    89 note, 161; by France, 55
    note, 241; by Hebrews, 220;
    by special act, 169; by
    states, 18, 85, 87, 102 note,
    126, 134, 258 f.; colonial,
    17; fees for, 174, 229, 232f.,
    245; fraudulent, 222 f., 242,
    245, 256 f.; methods of,
    227 f., 243; of Chinese,
    287; political committees
    of, 230 f.; progressive, 36,
    39 f., 66; wholesale, 224,
    229 f.
Naturalization Society of New
    York, 231.
New York, 260, 266, 269.

Niles Register, 185 f.
Oath of allegiance, 1, 2.
Oregon, 296.
Paupers, 193 f., 226, 263 f.
Petitions, 110 f., 122, 171 f.,
    192 f., 204, 215, 217 f.,
    247, 264 f., 277.
Pinckney, Charles, 139.
Pinckney's plan, 20.
Polacre Ship "Adams," case
    of, 139.
Privileges, 60, 287.
Publishing, 131, 205.
Randolph, Edmund, 18 f., 28.
Repatriation, 54 f., 159.
Revolutionary War, 5.
Rhode Island, 265, 280.
Seward, William H., 274, 276.
Slavery, 61f., 249, 289f., 295.
Suffrage, 37, 41, 76, 79, 253f.,
    280, 287, 292 f.
T. C. of Northumberland, 141.
Territories, 68 f.
Titles, 56 f.
Tories, 1, 3.
Twenty-one years' residence,
    198, 203, 215 f., 219, 247,
    256, 278 f., 293.
Vattel, 140.
Virginia, 134, 136, 150, 162.
Washington, George, 33, 66.
Webster, Daniel, 272.
Williams, Isaac, case of, 138f.
Women, 244, 272 f.
Wisconsin, 288.